BREATHE LIFE

BREATHE LIFE

PROPHETESS NEKESHIA L. GIBSON

Superior Publising LLC.

Contents

notes	ix
1	1
2	7
3	12
4	17
5	22
6	27
7	33
8	40
9	47
10	54
11	59
12	63
13	68
14	72

Copyright © 2020 by Nekeshia Gibson
All rights reserved. No part of this publication may be reproduced, distributed, or transmitted in any form or by any means, including photocopying, recording, or other electronic or mechanical methods, without the prior written permission of the publisher, except in the case of brief quotations embodied in critical reviews and certain other noncommercial uses permitted by copy-right law.
Superior Publishing LLC 2020 -Cedar Bluff, Mississippi

Breathe Life
By: Nekeshia L. Gibson

Front Cover by: Sherita Gayden, Houston, MS

Dedications

First, I want to give all praise and glory to the Highest od for allowing me to continue in His purpose. If He had not allowed the breath to stay in this body and speak over my life, none of this would be possible. All of this would never have come to be For that, Sir, I say thank you.

I want to say a special thank you to my children and express how incredibly grateful I am that they were chosen to be a par of my walk. Each of them brought something different, something individually, and something unique.

To my mother for being exceptionally strong and sticking with her convictions no matter what anyone says. Showing me how to push pass intimidation, lack of support, and saying what you believe to be the truth.

To my cousin/little brother, thank you for inspiring me and being there when I needed you the most. To my other cousin, whose more like a little sister, thank you for pushing me to become all that God has called me to be. As well as being a shoulder to lean on during each trial and transformation.

To my spiritual parents, thank you for the many prayers, the many talks, and the many encouraging words to propel me to continue pressing on despite what it looks like.

To my Apostle and First Lady, words cannot express how grateful I am that you are a part of my life. I appreciate every word every laugh, every chastisement, and every act of love you have shown me as I move into what God has for me. To my former leaders, I am profoundly grateful for how God used each of you to guide me, teach me, impart into me, and help me for this walk that has been placed before me. I am forever thankful to each of you. To my family, sisters, and brothers in Christ I love you all and thankful for every part played directly or indirectly in my life.

Finally, to my publicist, I give God the glory that you heard Him and took a chance with what He has placed in my heart to do. Words cannot express how truly humbled I am for such a God given heart to do this for a little ol' girl from East Missis-

sippi. Thank you so very much. I pray this book bless all that read and inspire each one to keep living. God has a plan created specifically for you! God Bless!
Prophetess Nekeshia L. Gibson

Introduction

One of the first miracles one experiences daily would be the capability of taking a breath. Waking up and still managing to breathe into our lungs another day of opportunities that are promised in the order they are promised to take place. Sometimes the realities are not what we would want them to be, but it does not limit the chances of them manifesting through our hopes. Hope that things will be different. Hope that it can get better. Hope that what was missing is now right before our face. Hope that this day will produce what our hearts so desperately desires, yet the world refuses to release into our grasp. Never once considering to be delayed does not mean we are denied. We are on a schedule not managed by man, but by a higher power who is soon to introduce Himself into our lives. The purpose of writing "Breathe Life" is to show that there is a reason behind every breathe I have taken in this life I am living. From the negative to the positive, each part played divine purpose to fulfill something beyond my scope of understanding to this time in my life. This book expresses the adolescent's thoughts that formed and then took on a form of life of its own. A life to tear down, destroy, dismantle, and ultimately eliminate from the very face of this earth.

But, there was a higher purpose, A purpose that had to be developed, planted, and nurtured for a life that was not my own. Showing that no matter how our lives in one moment can be so close to becoming a wisp of a memory for others, the end of what I felt was purposeless, to purposeful, after I chose to continue to breathe until I caught another breath.

I

Chapter One

The one thing that one is never told once entering into life is, "how your life is going to be." We are taught behavior at a young age, mannerism at a young age, how to address our elders and strangers, how to walk, how to talk, etc; but that one key part is something that we find out during the process of living it. Some live exceptional lives and feel nothing more is needed. Others live lives that could be more and strive to get it. Then there are those who desire more, hungering with a thirst to understand life and the acts that have molded what they knew or thought they knew. In this place is where my life began. A place that had much darkness with very little hope of accomplishing much due to the demons I fought on a daily basis. Some who read this will not understand that statement, but there are those who will connect. Life has many different mysteries attached to it. Those mysteries can either draw curiosity to determine when and how it is going to be; or it can cause one to ignore it without stretching into that place that has potential to cause some things to take place or shape within it. Once upon a time, I called that place ugly because I did not understand it and the feelings I was drawing from it was difficult to understand. Little did I think or even know that the small recesses of my mind carried a theory that was not created by the hands of man, but by one who knew more than I could ever think or perceive in this lifetime. In these next few chapters, I'm going to examine over the many different places my life took prior to the destination I am currently at. Even in this single place, I'm predestined for more than I can even imagine at this time, but the journey will be worth the

wait. Sometimes living in today can cause reflections of yesterday for it was during those times one is being made or rather yet created for the next day. For hope of today reflected off the desires of yesterday and can transcend over indefinite tomorrows. With that being the case, speaking peace consistently can do and bring remarkable results when you believe. It took many years for me to figure this out and, in all honesty, it is still a work in progress. Change is the one thing that can happen to anyone who desires it. Whether it is for the good or for the bad, it is possible. With change comes an awareness that can either dull the senses or heighten them. Depending on the person, the situations, and even the concept of life, not excluding the hope of it, change can determine many things concerning one. How effective is change? Let's examine that question to the heart. If one has a bad situation happen to them, how much of it would change the person, for example. Can the conclusion to this answer be determined by exactly the form of this "bad situation"? Now considering this same issue, what if the "bad situation" was a constant thing that seem to never get better? Can one then determine the outcome of that person due to the innumerous acts of "bad situation"? Just simple food for thought. If I looked upon all my yesterday's prior to finding The Lord, I can honestly say there were many bad days and unnumbered bad situations that almost molded my future, but then I breathed life. When this happened, everything changed. Causing this leader to become a follower for a greater goal. In order for you to understand what I mean, I have to paint a picture of the past for the understanding of the present, and the praise for the upcoming future.

    Born in 1974, in a small town in Central Mississippi, I am the eldest of two by my mother and the youngest of four by my father. Growing up, I never knew my father and the one person who held that position was my grandfather. I spent much of my youth with my grandmother and grandfather due to my mother almost always seeming to be at their house. After a while, it became comforting being around them, but I was more of a granddaddy's baby then anything. At the young age of five, my grandfather went into the hospital to have his leg removed. I did not know this at the time due to my age, but I remember my mother going to the old hospital to visit him leaving my sister and I in the car. I would lean out the window and shout "Hey Granddaddy" and see this arm lift in the window waving hello to me. After a few days, my sister and I were allowed to go in and visit my grandfather on one of the trips my mother took to visit him. I was too young to remember how many visits it was before I actually saw him, but it was not long afterwards before it was the last. I remember him being wheeled out into the hallway and running up to meet him throwing myself into his arm. Before I reached his arms, I remember seeing one of his leg and the space where his right leg use to be being gone. He smiled and introduced me to the nurse letting her know I was his granddaughter as he was attempting to get my baby sister to come to him too. I'm tickled as I remember her shaking her head and him calling her "red tail". That was the last time I saw my grandfather alive. My next memory is of him lying in a casket as the family went around viewing his body in the front of the church. Watching my grandmother crying on the front row caused my little mind to be confused as to why was everyone crying? Granddaddy was only sleeping, so I thought. I remember asking my mom during the burial why they were putting him in the ground, which caused my mom to cry even more. At that point, I knew even at the tender age of five that I would not see my grandfather any more. Little did I know how wrong I would be on that notion. After the service, everyone climbed into their cars and we all headed out to my grandparents' house. It was amazing to me how many people were at the house and they seemed to keep coming. Pretty soon, there were so many different vehicles in the yard to where there wasn't room for any of us kids to play. After a while, I decided to go sit outside to get away from all these adults and my eyes fell on my granddaddy's car. I use to be scared of that car because of the way it looked. It was long, black, and had the silver tips on the wings of the trunk. When I looked in the driver's window, I saw this man who looked very much like my grandfather smiling and looking back at me. When I blinked, he was gone and for a long time I stared at that car to see if I would see him again. I didn't. Finally, all the people started leaving and I became tired ready for bed. My mom decided to stay the night out at my grandparents' house with the rest of her brothers and sisters, which meant we were staying the night. My mom put me in the bed with my grandmother and I remember being upset about that. My grandmother snored really bad, leading me to point this out to my mom, but she would not bulge on her decision. I remember going to bed mad and I just knew I would not get any sleep before school. After laying there for several hours trying to sleep, my grandmother gave one of her rare pause in snores and I finally drifted off to sleep. I do not know how long I was asleep when I heard someone calling my name. I remember opening my eyes, hearing my name again, and looking at the end of the bed on the left side. Standing at the foot of the bed was a man in a black suite, white shirt, and black tie. He looked at me, smiled,

and then his eyes turned a red as if fire was coming out of them! I laid there shaking because he looked familiar, he looked just like my grandfather, but I was afraid. I closed my eyes tight and when I opened them again the man was gone. I screamed and screamed until the entire house was woken. Afraid that this man would appear again. By the time my mom made it to me, all I could do was cry and tell her about the man who looked like my granddaddy standing at the end of the bed. She smiled and told everyone "she saw daddy", but for me it did not feel that way. After a while, she put me in bed with her and I fell into a really deep sleep. The next thing I knew I was standing in the front of my grandparents' house with the entire family and my grandfather was there saying goodbye. I remember him hugging me, telling me he loved me, he would always be there for me when I need him in my heart, and finally goodbye. I asked him why he was leaving and he said he had to go. I looked up and a small piece of cloud floated down to his feet, he stepped on it, and the cloud started going up. While watching him go up, I noticed there were people standing in the sky. Hundreds and thousands of people were standing on shelves of clouds in the sky looking down at me while smiling. Tears were streaming down my face as I watch my grandfather disappear in the throngs of people and my little eyes opened to see I was dreaming. I sat up in the bed, heard my family in the kitchen talking, walked into the kitchen, and told everyone "granddaddy said bye". Everyone paused what they were doing at that moment, stared at me, with my mom being the first to break the silence with the question everyone was thinking. "What do you mean?" At that point, I told them my dream while

watching their reactions. Wondering if they would believe me. My mom smiled, my aunts cried, my uncles said nothing, and my grandmother cried more. Seeing these different reactions to what I said, I did not think I wanted to share anything that would make them sad, but I did not know that many more dreams, many more visitations, and many other things had just been opened to one at the young age of five. Much more would follow behind a life changing experience that had only just starting to begin.

2

Chapter Two

There are many different things that people remember about the childhood. Memories of games, toys, books, trips, summer vacation, and other events that took place during those times. Summer would be the one feature that any child or adult would say they had the best times; even when they knew those times would have to come to an end. The same can be said for my many different adventures growing up. From playing hide and seek with the other kids in my family to putting t-shirts on my head like hair, grabbing the brush, and singing in the mirror like it was a microphone. One of my most memorable moments would be the first time I heard Whitney Houston's song, "The Greatest Love of All." I fell in love with that song instantly and spent majority of the day waiting for the top 10 songs to play. Thinking back, I couldn't go a day sweeping without stopping and singing with the broom as my mic whenever one of her songs played. There are so many different memories that bring a smile to my face as I reminisce about those days, but just as there were good days there were also those days I considered terrifying. During those times, that is exactly how it felt for one so young with no knowledge to help me understand what was going on. Those emotions followed majority of my lifespan and contributed to many things that I endured because of it. At the tender age of 9 years old, I had my very first, what many would call, nightmare. I remember waking up on so many different nights due to these consistent dreams. In each of them, there was the same figure of a little green man who harassed me to the point that I would stay up late just so I would not dream at all. I ended up missing several days of school because I was unable to sleep. I remember one specific dream where he chased me around my bedroom and no matter how I tried, I could not find a door out of that room to escape for safety. It became so very bad for me that I was tired of not being able to sleep and it began to affect me mentally. My school life was just as bad as well as not being able to sleep. I was unable to make any friends and was the target of much "fun" that other children manage to have with me. I remember trying to fit in with the other kids or better yet the "popular" kids, but it was more of a humorous joke for them than a friendly experience for me. These experiences lasted until my junior year of school, but this I will discuss later on. Now you have to realize that with all these things happening to one at a young age, it can begin to take a toll on a child's self-esteem, image, and thoughts. I didn't speak to anyone about the mental stress I was under because I did not think anyone cared or wanted to hear about it. Being so young, I did not understand what was going on myself. Only that I was tired and I was afraid all the time not understanding why. After a while, another voice began to speak to me. Luring me to think as well as believe that no one cared about me and the only one who did was now deceased. Convincing me that maybe that was the answer. Causing me to think and feel that the only way I would be happy or escape what I was dealing with would be to forget this life to cross over to the afterlife with the person who left me. For several months, this particular voice spoke very convincingly to me. Having me look at all the people around me from my family, to my peers and explained to me that none of them cared if I lived or died. Strengthening its position that the one person who did love me was waiting for me to join him. Finally, one night, after being worn down that this was the best choice to make, at the age of 9, I made my first suicide attempt. I went into my grandmother's bathroom, opened up the cabinet above the sink, looking to see what pills were found in there. I know those who are reading are wondering how is it a 9-year-old child could possible know to take pills and kill themselves? That is a good question and can easily be answered. When you have an enemy, who knows how to speak, he also knows how to give directions as well. Never underestimate your opponent; especially when they consider you a threat and that is exactly what I was without knowing it at that time. I picked up a bottle of aspirins and just looked at it. The voice continued to speak. Encouraging me to take the pills and go be with my granddaddy. I looked into the mirror, looked into my own eyes, and cried. I remembered my youngest aunt knocked on the bathroom door, making me jump, and told me to

hurry up she needed to get in there. Placing the bottle back into the mirror, I was afraid that someone would know what I was thinking about doing. Walking into the bedroom, I sat down on the bed and stared at the television without comprehending what was on. A while later, my mom told my sister and I that it was time for us to go to bed. At that moment, I began thinking about getting on that bus with the other kids that lived on the road and another day the pun of other kids humiliating jokes. The final thought was the dreams that was always lurking, waiting for me to slip off into sleep. Only to awaken me shaking, afraid to close my eyes, and always feeling as if someone was there waiting for me to close my eyes once again. Then there was the voice, convincing me that all these things could end with just a few pills, water, and closing of my eyes one final time. At this point, I was convinced that the world was not worth living and the one who loved me was waiting on me to come be with him. I got out the bed, opened the bedroom door and told my mom I had to use the restroom when she asked why was I up. I went into the bathroom, opened the cabinet, and once again found the aspirins bottle in my hand. After a few seconds, I opened it and poured most of the bottle into my little hand. I remembered thinking about my granddaddy and how I really missed him. For me, he was my protection and I was most happy when I was with him. At this point, every pill in my hand went into my mouth with a hand full of water from the sink helping me to swallow each one of them. I remembered thinking that I would leave some for someone else in case they had a headache. Thinking of this now, I can smile because even then I thought about others. I wasn't concerned about my mom because she had my sister. I didn't have a father in my life, so that didn't fade me. Everyone else was not a concern for me at that point. I walked back to the bedroom, laid in the bed, and closed my eyes

for what I felt was the last time. Whispering under my breath, "I love you, momma" and closed my eyes. Believing, without a shadow of a doubt, that the voice, which had stopped talking at this point, was telling the truth that I would finally be with my granddaddy. I don't know exactly when I fell asleep, but I do remember the dream that came to me. I saw my granddaddy walking toward me and he told me, "Not yet." The next thing I remembered was waking up and seeing it was still dark outside. The entire house was quiet, outside of my grandmother's snoring, and my mother was lying beside me. The next thing I knew, I became horrible sick and my stomach began to cramp up in this excruciating pain. I jumped out the bed, ran to the bathroom, and began to heave everything up. Jumping out of that bed must have woke my mom up because she came into the bathroom where I was. She felt my forehead and told me to go lay down assuring me I did not have to go to school. I stared crying. Not because I wasn't feeling well, but because the voice promised me something and it did not happen. I laid there thinking and feeling trapped. What more could go wrong? Little did I know, at that young age, that much more was to come that I little expected, but how bad could it get? Right? It did not dawn on me that someone chose to breathe life in me once again, but during this time it was the one thing I could not comprehend. For my young mind was not developed as of yet.

3

Chapter Three

When it comes to adolescence years, experts claim that those are the most impressionable years with children. A time where many factors come into play as far as peer pressure, behavior, attitude, school, and mostly acceptance are pursued by many children. In this, I was not too different and desired to get along with the other children. Preteen years are the most difficult and I can say that due to the experiences I had. As well as some others that were dealing with the same issues. It is amazing the things children will do just to get others to like them. Even going so far as to getting in to trouble in class or becoming the class clown just to fit in some kind of way. In an effort to fit in, there were those moments that I really felt that if I do silly stuff, my peers would accept me for who I am. That did not happen. At the age of 11, I was in my last year of middle school, but little had change over the years. I remember my mother getting a position in the cafeteria, so I got a chance to see her every day. It didn't bother me that my mom was working at my school, but eventually this became another "joke" for my peers to use against me. I remember one time, during class, one of my peers snuck over to my seat to tell me what another class member had stated about my mom. Going so far as to "politely" demonstrate what the other class member had did while the other people, who were part of the "joke", in class watched for my reaction. I didn't say anything. I looked back down at my assignment, continued writing, but my heart was severely hurt. Why would you make fun of my mom? I couldn't understand. How could kids be so cruel to another, but these were the people I called my friend. It was so very hard getting up every morning, 5 days during the week, and going to sit amongst a group who absolutely enjoyed hurting me. Just for a laugh. Eventually, I became more withdrawn, with no desire to show my hurt to any of them. Lying to them just to get them to like me even for a sliver of a moment. Things did not get any better and my young emotions could not comprehend what was wrong with me that people made fun of me? I remember during that time, I had a teacher that everyone was afraid of. She was known as being hard, mean, and did not mind hurting your feelings. On several occasions, I was the target of the day; including the laugh of the entire class. On numerous occasions I would deliberately sink down in my seat to avoid this teachers eye. One specific memory used to be difficult to think of and I avoided remembering my past as much as possible. As I'm writing these words, even now, my thoughts are flooded with the moments and thoughts of the ridicule I endured. Once I woke up late and almost missed the bus. I rushed to get ready and didn't realize that I forgot to put on any antiperspirant until after I got on the bus. It was supposed to have been cold that day, so my mom laid out a sweater for me to wear with my jeans. It didn't take long for me to realize it was going to be hot, so I consciously thought I would not do anything that would cause me to sweat. Lo and behold this did not work. I was so embarrassed that I did not try to move because I knew this would be a prime opportunity for the others to really target me. After trying to avoid my peers' jokes, it ended up being my teacher who stirred up the "fun". With tears in my eyes, I made a promise to myself I would not go back to that school or that class ever again. For weeks, I pretended to be sick to get out of going to school. At one point, I had contracted the mumps and I was so happy to have it. Eventually I got better, so I had to think of other reasons to avoid this class. Finally, one day, my mom received a call from the school telling her if I did not come to school I would failed. I couldn't face that school! I promised I would never go back! I was willing to die to keep from going. My mom ended up making me go and that dreaded day was upon me. I remember walking into the class and the teacher stating very loudly, "look who has decided to come back! I don't know why, you're not going to pass" and everyone laughing at what she said. I walked to my seat, sat down, dropped my head, and began to cry. Only to endure more insults and jokes from the one who was supposed to provide me with an education. I made up in my mind that if I was forced to return to that class, I would surely take my life. I refused to go through this again. My little mind and heart could not take it anymore. I remember thinking, "if my mom loved me, she would not make me go." That day, during lunch, my mom looked at me while she was serving me and asked me what was wrong? I didn't respond, just shook my head, and walked over to a seat to be alone. She watched me the entire time in the lunch room and I really believe my teacher was paying close attention to this interaction. I say this because I watched my teacher walk over and start talking to my mom. Acting as if nothing had happened or ever happened; which was a total insult to me all the way around. That night at home, my mom asked me again what was wrong and I continued to claim nothing telling her I didn't feel well. She pressed until she finally got through letting me know she was still sending me to school the next day. Causing me to cry, beg her to let me stay home and in the end attempting to take my life with pills once again. This time, I didn't hear a voice to convince me. I just needed to get out, away from these horrible feelings. I was not willing to endure any more pain or rejection from these people. I did not desire this or want this any longer. I went into the bathroom, opened up the cabinet, grabbed whatever pill bottles was in it, and took as many as I could. I wanted it to be over. My next memory was waking up in the hospital and seeing my mom next to me. The look of not understanding reflecting off her face and even more the hurt that I had done this. I was quiet much of the time and really did not say anything. Eventually, I went home and had to face the questions I knew were coming. The main one: why? We were still living with my grandmother at the time, so the entire family heard everything. Each one giving their opinion on what needs to be done. The end results being my mom calling the principal and telling him everything; including how all of this had made me sick. Being young and at this age, it was very easy to be intimidated. I did not know how or what reactions would come behind my revealing all this to my mom. I just knew that I had finally spoken out and the pressure was less than what it was. It didn't go away completely, but it was easier to deal with than where it used to be. The next phase I remember going through was fear. Fear of the repercussions that would come behind telling what was taking place within that classroom. The principal informed my mom that if I didn't miss any more days when I returned to school, they would not hold me back. My mother talked this over with me and agreed. Though I dreaded that day, eventually I returned to school and approached what had become to be known as doom to me. Stepping into the class, the teacher welcomed me back and ended it just like that. It was very uncomfortable for me, but I was able to come every day with little to no interactions (outside of school work) with the teacher. Now don't get me wrong, those days after my incident weren't all that bad. During that time, I met someone who would become one of my closest friends for a very long time and eventually my sister. I remember walking into the cafeteria during lunch break and my mom observing me closely before asking how was I doing. After responding to her, she pointed toward one of the tables and asked me did I see the little girl sitting over there. Glancing over to the spot she was pointing out, I looked at the girl with vague curiosity. My mom informed me that she was a cousin and she wanted me to go over to sit with her. At this, I rejected the idea. I had more than enough of getting to know any more people; especially my peers. My mom pretty much threatened me with not being able to watch television if I didn't; provoking a "I can't believe you're doing this to me" look as I slowly approached the table. When I sat down, I looked at this person my mom had me go sit with and wondered why this was happening to me. I looked at this big head, big eyes, girl who was sitting alone and staring at her food. I glanced at my mom and she beckon for me to say something. Causing me to wonder why I had to sit with her and why she was sitting alone. I finally said hey and she quietly responded back without lifting her head to even glance at me. Who was this strange girl and why did my mom find it so important for me to talk with her? As I sat there looking at her, she finally looked up, and for a split moment I saw something I never thought I would see. The same sadness and pain that I was feeling, she had that same look on her face! Seeing this, it prompted me to introduce myself and she slowly followed with her name. We gradually began to eat, still observing one another, and eventually finishing to return to class. From that day forward, we always manage to find each other in the cafeteria and made room when the other walked up. It became a strong bond, but like every relationship, there came storms. When those storms come, it can tell you many things if the maturity is there before its broken. I never expected anything to last; especially friendship. So when it comes along and it's the real thing; the only thing that could separate it is death. Neither one of us was expecting this to happen any time soon, but it is strange how some things don't always pan out the way we think; even when we perceive it. It's in those moments, we are tested in many ways where we are opened.

4

Chapter Four

There is an old saying that I have heard many of my elders speak on several occasions growing up; "You can't teach an old dog new tricks." There is another one that I find my personal favorite, "Actions speak louder than words." I never knew who spoke this, but I've carried this with me for a very long time due to hearing my elders say many things to me. I was taught that the actions of a man say a lot of things about them, but the funny thing about this that I never truly understood was what if the actions weren't real? Can this still apply to that person? This was a question that stuck to me for a while and later on in my adult years, I found out the answers. Every age brings a different lesson. From learning how to behave in polite society to learning how to hide from those who were closest to you. The latter I learned how to perfect from the various oppositions I faced on a regular basis. I cherished every person The Lord sent my way that I knew were my dearest friends and to this day, that has not changed. By the time I turned 15 years old, much around me had changed. No longer was it pony tails, lace skirts, swing sets, or playing makeup with my dolls. Now the peers around me were dressing different, wearing makeup, and seeking the attention of the opposite sex. How quickly things had changed on the outside, but nothing felt different on the inside. Seeing that everything had evolved, I decided to evolve with it. I had made some friends and hung out with them every day during school. I still wasn't allowed to go out, but I was allowed to have a young man come over to see me. Sitting here reflecting on those moments where I could do thing differently, I'm pretty much sure a lot of my choices still surrounded being accepted by those around me. I had gotten to a point where I was very much self-conscious about my looks. I always felt that I was too dark and there was nothing about me that would be considered pretty. I would stand in the mirror trying to do something different about myself, but the results never made me feel any different about myself. It's amazing the things that goes through a young girl's mind about herself and how she demoralizes herself more than anyone else could. Since I couldn't be as pretty as my peers, I began to do a lot of things to be part of the in crowd. Skipping school, class clown, detention, and suspension became the norm for me a lot in those days. The only time I felt any peace during those times was the moment I joined band. I grew up listening to my aunt play her flute and there was something about that sound that inspired me to learn how to play that instrument. I use to sneak into her bedroom, after she left for work or going over town, and try to play it before she made it home. I remember the band director telling me I would not be able to play it because of the raindrop on my top lip, but I refused to accept any other instrument. I picked up a flute and specifically stated I wanted to play this instrument. The director wiped the instrument, handed it to me, and gave me a look that reflected doubt that any notes would come from it due to the rain drop on my lip. I remember thinking about how my aunt use to play in her room and how I truly desired to play this instrument. I placed the flute to my lip, closed my eyes, and played the highest notes that the director had heard from anyone who attempted to play before me. I remember opening my eyes and looking at the director. At the memory of the look on his face, I can still smile as I think on it. On that day, I proved that I was capable of doing what I was told I could not do. For the first time, I proved someone wrong in their assumption of me and one more than one occasion I held the first chair for this instrument. It always fell between another young lady and myself. That is a moment in time I can say I was very proud of myself and wish that this was something that carried over to other areas of my life. Unfortunately, it didn't. During those class periods, I lost myself in time. In the music I had come to love so very much. There were so many times I wished that class would last forever. It didn't matter to me that the band director shouted all the time. All that matter was I was playing my flute and I was happy about something I was doing right. Walking out of that class brought reality back to me. A reality that I wanted to leave and never deal with again. Walking out of that class brought on another personality. One I adopted just to fit in. I was no longer the girl who could play the flute, but the girl who would put on an act to show the others I'm just as cool as they were. It never dawned on me that others could have been feeling the exact same way as I was. As I reflect back on those days, I never considered that the very people I was trying to hang out with were going through similar pressures as I was. These same people had gained an image or reputation. There is more pressure to hold up to an image greater than a person realizes until they became part of it. As I look at some of the children in this world now, I can relate to much of what they are dealing with and going through on a regular basis. No one teaches you to be tough. No one teaches you to fight. No one tells you that you could be bullied today or better yet you could be the target of one. When you face those moments in your life, the only thing you try to understand is "why". What have I done to cause people to treat me this way? This question is one that never leaves the thoughts of the one going through this. The worse part about this entire scenario is not the person who is doing it, but the adults that watch it happen along with participating in it. For many this may amaze you, but even during my time of growing up there were those "adults" who were "teachers" that participated with those "children" who were bullies. Curious how the same issues are still around today except now many children, who have taken their lives due to this issue, has given face to the word bulling. My thoughts and prayers goes out to these families. The one thing I could never comprehend would be why some of the adults, in my life during that time, treated me just as awful as my peers. I was too afraid to tell my mother, so I chose to skip school than to go to that particular class. I remember my mother getting a call from the school informing her that I was never counted in that class, but showed for the others. When my mother confronted me, I told her the truth. I did not want to go into that class to be picked on and cursed out in front of everyone just for a laughed. My mom asked me some questions, called up to the school, and made arrangements to meet with the principal. I was hopeful that the teacher would not find out it was me, but on the day of the meeting she was in the office as well. I was terrified of this teacher and found myself stuttering when I was asked questions. During the meeting, I realized that the principal and my teacher had gotten together to form a good case against me. I told my mom that it was not true, but she did not believe me. Right there, in front of the teacher and principal, my mom paddled me. A piece of me died at that moment. A piece that used to care, but no longer did. I realize now, I never forgave my mother for what she did. The look on the teacher's face was a smugness that let me knew she would get even. I had no choice, but to return to that class. My teacher ensured I was uncomfortable in every way and in that she very well succeeded. Time has a way of showing one things once some distance is placed between it. The gaps are understood as maturity sets in, but during that time it only brought anger.

An anger that did not care nor tried to. Darkness forms and takes many different shapes.

One has to know what to do in order to defeat it; especially one who is still young and

impressionable. This was something I had not been taught and would have to find out on my

own.

5

Chapter Five

Reflecting back on the 80's and the 90's, I must admit that these were the times where many things were coming forward that would forever be called "classic" for my age group. From movies, to clothes, to introduction of new foot ware, hairstyles, and most importantly, (at that time) music. Ahh, yes! The music that many of us grew up with in our families and then being introduced to what our taste had formed. I remember the first time I heard Keith Sweat, Jodeci, New Edition, SWV, Tevin Campbell, HI FIVE, Gerald Levart, GUY, and the infamous Blackstreet. There were other groups out there that eventually came out, but late 80's, early 90's, these artists were bringing a music similar to what I grew up with, but different enough to be for my times. Summer time brought about many adventures and late nights of laughter like none other. There was a particular club that everyone was always riled up about getting to during the weekends. The fact that I was still unable to attend these weekend "functions" due to my age was excruciating to deal with; especially when many of the people I had connected to were able to go without some of their parents caring. A lot of the reasons for that was because majority of the parents were in similar facilities themselves. Just saying. Even though I was unable to go to these spots on the weekend, I was still able to have people over and this I did on a regular basis. During the year of 1990, I had gotten to the point where the elders of this world would call "fast". I had begun to circulate in my peer group and built

up a confidence that was more outer than it was inner. Though I wasn't allowed to date or have a boyfriend at the age of 14, things were different when I wasn't at home. After turning 15, I was allowed to have boyfriends, as well as company, but I was still not allowed to go much of anywhere still. This was something I found really hard to accept and I expressed this through a rebellious attitude I made a point of demonstrating on a daily basis. I wondered on numerous occasions if anyone would ever understand me or would I ever gained that one friend I could talked to. I must admit that I had several people I laughed or talked with, but there was still a part of me that wanted much more. Not long after thinking this way, my best friend/cousin ended up living with us. I was so happy and excited she was there. We sat up talking, singing, talking on the phone with boys, and many other acts young teens did growing up. In the house, we were normal teen girls. Outside of the house brought a different personality altogether. I remember one time we invited some guys over and sat outside on the porch just enjoying ourselves. It's amazing how such small moments can bring a smile to one's face, but as always there was darkness lurking in the background. Biding its time to invade and cast its shadows on any type of light managing to stream through. Two months after moving in with my family, my cousin, who had come to be my sister, was made to leave our home. I remember the emotions that flooded my heart and my thoughts to see her being pulled away from our family. Knowing that the stability she had begun to form in her heart was once again stirring up issues that we would one day have to face on several occasions. I walked around depressed for a very long time and hurt when I found out she had been sent away to a boarding school several miles away. I never got the chance to say good-bye to her, but I knew we would see each other again. Summer had come to an end and sweet 16 was right over the horizon. Even though this was the moment I had been waiting on, it was bitter sweet without my sister with me. There were so many things I was dealing with and had no one I felt that I could share this with. A few weeks before my birthday, something amazing happened. I actually met a new friend. This time, they were completely opposite to my sister/cousin and, unbelievably, it was a guy. When I first met him, I found him very much annoying and really did not like him in the beginning. He was playful, acted very silly, said the most inappropriate things, and was just plain strange. Even though he had all these qualities that would normally make me avoid a person, for some reason he kept approaching me. I remember asking him why do you act this way? What can you possible get from doing what you do? He looked at me and said, "because I know I get on your nerves and I'm not going to stop until you like me." The look on my face must have spoken everything I was feeling because he laughed so hard at the expression on my face. I remember thinking I would never like him and before I knew it I had come to seek him out whenever I sat amongst the people I had come to hang out with. After a while, it became almost natural for us to be together. To share the love as a sister and brother would. He never approached me in any way that made me uncomfortable and that made our relationship even greater. I had found someone else to fill that void once again and I cherished every moment we had together. Eventually he started coming over to my house and my mom informed us that we were related. I was so happy to know that we were family and made sure everyone knew we were. It became almost an expectation for everyone that if he was not at my home on the weekend, I would be at his. The one thing that amazed me at that time was the fact that my mother did not mind this at all. She had come to love him like a son and his parents was pretty much use to seeing me out there as well. A lot of people did not approve of our friendship, but we laughed continuing to enjoy our closeness. At one point, we became each other Pandora's box. Sharing secrets and situations that we had not told anyone. He once told me something that really rattled my thoughts about when/how he would die and I made him promise not to say it again. I can still hear his sniggering, telling me "alright", and continuing on with our conversations. That night, I had one of my dreams that were constant at that point, and I woke up feeling drain, afraid. Unsure if I should say something or keep it to myself. I had started noticing that many of my dreams were happening and my small mind could not understand this. There were many dreams I had shared with him, but this would be one of the first I didn't. Like many other things, I kept it bottled up and did not want to ever share this with anyone. I remember him calling me that night, asking me why I hadn't called, and me quickly saying I had been busy. He attempted to question me, but after a while he eventually changed the subject. I remember thinking, how much I loved my best friend. I knew this relationship would never be replaced.

We began talking about my upcoming birthday and what I wanted to do to celebrate. Immediately I let him know I was coming out to his house for us to go to the club and he agreed that he would be there as well. Thinking back, I use to call what I saw come to pass as déjà vu. A moment in time where I saw these things before not realizing just how accurate my dreams had come to be. It could be a scary thought when you see or know things without anyone ever having said one solitary word about it. Making one almost speechless. Never the less, destiny has its designated course and one cannot run from where they're going versus where they have been.

6

Chapter Six

There are many different parts of life that everyone comes to anticipate during our course through it. Some anticipate that new outfit that they're going to get from that clothing store that no one has heard of just yet. There are those who anticipate that phone call from that special one at that moment. Then there are those waiting for that special age where things are supposed to be different. That special age that everyone talks about and remembers for the actions that took place when it came. Yes, I'm talking about that sweet 16. That oh so wonderful age where one is in between childhood and adulthood. There were even movies created about that particular age to mark or better yet commemorate its special time in a teenager's life. I remember watching one of these movies called Sixteen Candles starring Molly Ringwald. A young lady preparing for her oldest siblings wedding day, having her 16 birthday forgotten by her loved ones, and loving one of the young men in her school from a distance. The ending bringing her and this distant love together for the best birthday celebration her heart could imagine. The movies can truly inspire an imagination toward what one would like to have as a memory for that moment. The only drawback would be the fact that reality can quickly place the undeniable truth over such a perfect illusion. I had finally reached that age that I was so desperately and impatiently waiting on. Happy with all the perks known to come with it as far as going out on a date, to the club, and having a curfew that allowed me to have fun for a good while before going home. I remembered going out for the first time on my birthday weekend. I didn't go far. Just out to my cousin's house and to the club that they owned. I remember going into it for the first time that night while it was filled to the top with people of various ages. My eyes were quenched so tight trying to see the people through the smoke and the very small room spaced between each person. The music was loud, but the voices within were even louder. Causing me to talk louder to my cousin just so he could hear me. I remember his mom seeing us and waving us over to the bar. Speaking to me and asking us what we were up to. We both laughed and he told her it was my birthday; even though my birthday had been earlier that week. She wished me a happy birthday and told us she better not catch us drinking. We both gave our promise that we wouldn't, (with neither us being aware of the small bottle of alcohol my cousin had swiped from behind the bar), and walked around the club just being nosey. After a while, I told him I was ready to go after seeing that it really wasn't all that I had expected it to be. We decided to go back to his house and basically watch television as well as making phone calls to other peers. At one point, his brother and his brother's girlfriend came to the house to get ready for the club as well. I remember sitting in the living room area watching everything taking place between them and waiting for them to leave. After a while, they left and my cousin walked into the room with his drink in his hand. He sat down beside me and asked me what did I want to do? Causing me to simply shrug my shoulder and say whatever he wanted to. He looked at me, looked at the drink in his hand, and stated plainly, "your mom is not going to kill me for giving you something to drink." We both laughed and started talking until someone knocked on the door before walking in. The moment I looked at the person walking through the door, I really didn't pay attention to the others with him. I didn't know him, but my cousin definitely did from the way they were acting with each other. From there on, there was a small gathering at my cousin's house that lasted close to the time the club closed. We both knew that if his parents came home, caught all these people in their house, they would definitely have a fit. So everyone disbanded to go home or to the hangout spot for the remainder of the night. As for me, it was time to go home. My cousin and these friends gave me a ride back to my house. Preparing to drop me off before heading to their designated spot, but I did get a chance to ask my cousin for this one particular person's name. After getting this name, I remember telling my cousin to call me. There were some questions I needed ask before saying anything. Watching me closely, he agreed to call, but claimed he already knew what I was going to say. That night, I laid in the bed and thought that my 16 birthday wasn't all that bad. It wasn't as good as the movies projected it to be, but it was still okay for the real world. Closing my eyes, I could still hear the music in my ears, hear the laughing of the people, and smell the different fragrancies that swarmed around the club. Allowing me to experience what so many of my peers had called fun and prepared for every weekend. True, I didn't get the thrill of all of all of this like so many of them did, but I got a chance to enjoy my weekend with one of my closest friends. That made that moment even more special and continues to hold a spot in my heart. Late that night or better yet early that morning around 3 am, my phone rung waking me up. I had my own phone line helping not to wake the house, but in the still of the night it didn't matter. Saying hello in a very deep sleep voice, I heard my cousin on the other end telling me to wake up. Slowly coming to, I asked him what was wrong and he begin to tell me about some girl he had met. I couldn't believe! He actually woke me up to tell me something like that? This was something I did verbalize to him and instantly I heard that sniggering on the other end. After laughing at me, he explained he had something to tell me. That the person, who had caught my interest at his home, had also informed him that they were interested too. At this point, my eyes popped opened and I sat up in the bed. Demanding that he tell me everything. It's funny how adrenaline works in the human body. Operating at a time of true excitement or out of tremendous fear. At that point, I believed I experienced both. Enough so that I couldn't go back to sleep until later that morning. Waking up, I was all smiles for the day. I actually felt pretty and was happy in my skin. Believing that the year may turn out to be a great one. Never expecting the hand I was about to be dealt. I never got the chance to really get to know this person that caught my interest. For some reasons, it just did not happen, but the future was still in the making. It's true that one should never say never when the future has not come into the picture as of yet. A few weeks after turning 16, I met another young man. This one was older and in a different school. Everyone knew him, many of the girls liked him, but some kind of way I caught his eye. I remember the first time I met him. It was after school and I had decided to walk home that day with a couple of the girls I had become friends with. The bus he was on was about to pass by and all of a sudden the young man head was hanging out the window. I remember my friends laughing and telling me he is looking at you. Asking me if I knew him. After telling them no, they quickly informed me of who he was and just how popular he was at that time. I didn't think for a moment that this guy was actually looking at me and so really didn't take to heart what they were saying. The next day, my friends convinced me to walk home again with them. After a while, I agreed and we started our log track down the road. Once again, this bus passed us, but this time the driver had to stop to let other kids cross the road before it could pull off. Again this head came out the window, looked me in the eyes, and asked me what was my name. I remember thinking "he really is talking to me," gave him my name, and was instantly given his. After giving him my name, finding out his, I was asked for my phone number and asked if it was alright if he called me. I remember smiling while I answered his questions tickled at the way he was reacting. I had never seen anyone act like that about me and it really made me feel special in many ways. Later that day, I received my first phone call from this young man and oh, how wonderful it was to have someone so very interested in me. Someone that many of my peers were interested in, but he found me interesting. We talked for a very long time on the phone that night and I found it enduring how he shared many things with me. Who would have thought that a young man this age carried such deep thoughts? Who would have thought he would be willing to share those thoughts with me? This made me feel so special and little by little he was luring me in. After a couple weeks of talking on the phone, as well as sending each other notes by our peers, he asked me to be his girlfriend. I was thrilled that someone considered popular would actually want to date a person like me. Of course the natural response to this was yes with very little hesitation with it. I remember inviting him over that weekend to meet my mom and actually having a face to face conversation. Happiness was not the word to describe that moment for me. Little did I know that there is a side of man that can bring about many acts to form a person's character as well as those that can inflict much damage to another person's will. You really do not know the doors that you allow to open or the doors that should stay closed. When it comes to the matters of the heart, sometimes the mind can lose its will altogether, but even that in itself can be difficult; especially when the emotion fear walks in. Love is a powerful emotion. One that can bring much joy into any relationship when its real. The one thing that no one told me was the dangers it could bring as well. A danger that can sometimes be life threatening if one is not built up to live. In that, survival becomes essential to breathe.

7

Chapter Seven

In the beginning, man was created by God. Man was given permissions to name all the animals that God had created and thus he did as he was told. When God saw that man did not have a companion of his own, God then caused man to sleep in order to take from him a rib to create woman. A companionship that was described in the bible for all to read, acknowledge, and seek. It sounds so simple once you really understand what the Almighty was giving examples of. The only thing about this would be is this concept truly taught to those too young to understand what they are getting into versus what they should wait upon. Thinking back now, I did not know what it really meant to be in a relationship. During that time, it was all fun and games. Then there are those moments when there is no fun and another meaning comes into development altogether. A meaning, I'm sorry to say, that many young people deal with on a daily basis. Causing fear and shame to take away the laughter that use to be a permanent fixture on a young person's face. There are those who say that people can become older than their time. This I believe is true. Some can go through many issues in their life that produces a tiredness. A tiredness that seems constant no matter what they do or try to overcome it. Being a teenager, one looks at relationships as something that is frequent and can change on a weekly basis. No one truly seeks to be in one area for long, but there were those rare occasions where to meet young and stayed together for a lifetime. Those are what I called amazing to see two last beyond the expected. To them, I applaud. For others, it was still fun and exciting to date a person we liked. This is how I felt after meeting this older guy and finding we had a lot in common. It was rare to find someone with the interest I had, so to me this was a perfect match. After meeting my family, the weekend came for me to meet his mom. I was so excited and nervous at the same time. I did not know what she would think about me and I really wanted her to like me. I took special care in getting ready that day and I wanted him to be proud when he introduced me to her. I already knew one of his siblings, we were friends in school, and this was another plus for me. I really believed that with two on my side, his mom would really come to like me. I remember pulling up into the yard with him and him walking over to open the door for me. I looked around their yard and thought it was really nice, but I did not see myself living in the country ever again. Walking up to the front door, he looked at me and asked me was I ready? I nervously nodded my head and followed closely behind him as we entered into the house. His mom was walking out of the kitchen and I remember thinking she's so tiny! She had this small smile on her face as she extended her hand out to shake mine while he introduced her. Not long after greeting each other, I became really relaxed around her. She was a sweet lady and she made me feel quite at home. I looked over at him and he smiled nodding his head. I had passed the mother's inspection! We talked for a while, me answering her questions, and soon we went to his room to listen to music. She specifically informed him to keep his door opened causing me to laugh and shake my finger at him. I remember walking down the hall and looking at the different pictures that were lining the wall. He stopped and told me who each person was and also showed me every award he had accomplished. Walking into his room, I looked around examining everything that was out in the open, and really not expecting to see very much. Sitting down in a chair, he began showing me all his music and asking me did I want to watch a movie? I agreed and sat back in the chair. Thinking, "this feels more like being home than anything else." A few seconds later, his brother came to the door and I smiled happy to see him. We were good friends and he always made me laughed with the jokes he was continuously speaking. I remember telling him to come in, but seeing the hesitation on his face. I looked over to his brother asking if it was okay. He said it was, but the atmosphere had suddenly changed. There was a chill in the air and I couldn't understand that. Looking back at my friend, I watched as he glanced at his brother and politely decline to come in. I couldn't understand at that moment what had happened, but I knew some kind of exchange took place without me being aware of it. After he left the doorway, I looked at my boyfriend and asked him what was that all about. The next thing I knew, my boyfriend facial features changed and he took on another look altogether. No longer was there this warm shy look, but one of sternness anger. He told me slowly he did not want me hanging out with his brother and forbid me to even talk to him. We were not "allowed" to be around each other, unless he was giving me a note from him, and if he wasn't home when I called, I was not to stay on the phone talking to his brother. We could talk when we were around him, but when my boyfriend was not present, no. He explained to me he wanted me to go tell him. I couldn't believe this! What was going on and who was this person speaking? Sitting there, looking in his face, I remember thinking this can't be serious. I automatically laughed and told him stop playing. I found out in an instant he wasn't. The next thing I knew, the right side of my face was stinging from the hand he quickly brought across my face. I sat there stunned. Did this really just happen to me? Did this sweet, kind, soft voiced gentleman just slap me across the face? It wasn't possible! I remember looking at him with total disbelief and jumping to my feet demanding he take me home. He looked at me and very nicely informed me I wasn't going anywhere until I ate what his mother had cooked. Unbelievable! Was I just informed that I was stuck out there until I ate? I let him know right then I wasn't hungry and would eat when I got home. The next instant, I was pushed hard into the chair and told with a hardness that if I did not keep my voice down as well as calm down, I would pay for it later on. Immediately fear rose up on me like never before. I could feel the danger I was in and there was nothing I could do about it. I quickly thought about telling his mom, but he informed me what would happened if I did. It was as if he could see my thoughts. Could read exactly what I was planning on doing. I sat back in the chair in total disbelief trying to understand how I got into this place? I had seen many people my age brutalized by other guys in our peer group, but never once did I think this would happen to me. I remembered all the big talk I had made if someone did this to me, but none of that confidence was coming up at that moment. The fact was I was afraid. This person was stronger than me plus anything could happen between there and home. Survival is an instant state that the mind goes into. It helps you to make the right choices at that moment until you get to safety. I truly believe that the small voice instructing me was of a higher power. Telling me to stay calm and it will soon be over. So that is what I did. I was instructed to go into the bathroom and fix my face. To be sure I came out smiling. I ended up bumping into his brother, my friend, in the hallway, but I quickly turned my head and walked back into the bedroom. I remember the look on my friend's face. As if he knew what had happened. The next thing I knew, he was calling my boyfriend out into the hallway and they began to argue. I sat there listening and could hear my friend asking his brother what had he done to me? I remember my boyfriend telling him it was none of his business. That I was his girlfriend and he knew he liked me. Hearing that, I was shocked, but it eventually faded away. The only thing I knew was I needed to get home. After a while, his mom called us out for dinner and we made our way to the kitchen table. I remember walking in a daze. Attempting to smile and make light conversation, but my heart was filled with fear. To this day, I believe his mom figured out what happened because she politely told him take me home. She smiled and hugged me. Told me I was welcome to come out anytime I wanted. Immediately I saw the sadness behind the smile. As if she had been in the same spot I was currently walking in, but I was determined that this walk would not continue. I looked at my friend, gave him a small smile, and he lifted his hand in a gesture of goodbye. Walking to the car, it was amazing how I was able to not run to safety. As he started the car, I remember thinking that I would never see this house again nor be in his company. After making it a distance down the road, the car began to slowly stop. I remembered looking over at him, wondering what was wrong with the car, and suddenly his hand went across my face. What in the world was going on? What caused this hateful act? I immediately started crying out of fear and pain. He informed me that he did not like the fact that I did not thank his mother for dinner and he was taking me back for me to complete this. He let me know that if I did not do it right I would not make it home until I did. The next thing I knew, he got out of the car and walked over to my side opening the door. He told me to get out the car and my heart started racing. Not knowing what the person, who was now a stranger to me, was about to do once I did. I slowly climbed out the car, thinking I would run if I have to, and moved to the side without touching him at all. He grabbed my hand and slowly pulled me to him. With the soft smile that was so familiar. He pulled me into his arms and informed me he was only training me to be the perfect girlfriend and eventually wife. I remembered being puzzled. Who in the world was this person? It was like I was dating two people in one body. How could the sweet soft spoken person, holding me so lightly, have a monster lurking in him? I couldn't understand. Getting back in the car, he turned around driving back to his house, and opened the door for me to get out. His mother must have been looking out the window because she came out on the porch asking him why he brought me back and him responding I had something to say to her. She looked at me closely and I knew she saw the truth. I apologized for not complimenting her on her dinner and thanked her for inviting me to share it with them. She looked at me, looked at him, grabbed my hand and told me there was nothing to apologize for. She looked at him and pointedly told him "take her home." He smiled and told her he would lying that I insisted to come back to tell her that. The look on her face told me many things, but the main thing being she knew it was a lie. Getting back into the car, I began to do something I had not done in a long time. I prayed. I asked God please let him take me home. Don't let him stop again. On the way home I was silent. The only thing I wanted was to get out that car. All the way to my house, he was telling me how he was going to pick me up every Saturday for me to spend the day with him and his family. In my mind, I was adamantly rejecting any notions of seeing him again. Pulling up into my yard, I restrained myself from jumping out of his car and running for dear life. Afraid he would follow behind me. He kissed my hand, told me he would call me later, and walked me to the door like the perfect gentleman. Making it into the house, I immediately went into my room, stretching across the bed, and cried. I had been through so much already and now adding this was truly a heavy burden for one so young to bear. I stayed in my room the remainder of the night and came out very little the next day. School the following week was as usually, but much of the spark I had was diminished. I remember my friends asking me how was my date and me saying very little to appease their interest. I remember seeing his brother, my friend, and turning going in the other direction. One day, in the hallway, he pulled me to the side and asked me what had his brother done to me? I never truly answered his question, but he told me that had fought that same night. He explained to me that he only saw me as a friend and he was not going to let anyone treat me this way; especially his brother. At this I cried and told him thank you. I knew then I had to end this horrible relationship. On Saturday, he showed up like he said he would and I remember watching out my bedroom window. I had decided to tell my mom what had happened, so my mother and family met him at the door. She politely informed him I was not going anywhere with him and he was never to come to her house again. I watched this soft face, soft voice turned very cynical. There was a smugness on his face as he looked at my mom, turned and walk to his car. I cannot explain the relief that came over me seeing him pull out of our driveway. I never heard from him again and neither did I attempt to contact him after that. The one thing I promised myself was I would never go through that again. The damages that comes from physical abuse can be horrible, but life was just beginning.

8

Chapter Eight

The one thing that I have heard many people say for as long as I can remember would be "your attitude will take you a long way." Another one would be "be careful how you treat others, you never know who you're going to need." For both of these sayings, I can attest that they are true sayings. When one is young, depending on the person themselves as well as their up bring, attitude and values can be within them. It is just a matter of how it comes up and come out. Many times, people feel that parents are responsible for their child's behavior. In many cases this can be true, but there are those cases where the parents are training the child in the right way to go even when they do not demonstrate it in public. Thus peer pressure. Now do not take this in the wrong context. Behavior is truly something that is defined by the parents and re-enforced through them as well, but there are those incidents where peer pressure as a greater influence versus the values that a child learns through those closest to them. It doesn't leave the mind of the one carrying it, but there are those times where the desire to be "part of the group" can carry more weight than the teachings; especially with adolescents. Growing up in a single-parent home is different in more ways than those of a two-parent. There are the same rules, the same rewards, and the same punishments as those of a two-parent. Even though these are the same, it doesn't bring on the same respect as having that missing figure there in the home. When this is the case, the single-parent end up having to balance both position to get that respect they rightfully deserve. In this area is where I fell when it came to being a child of a single-parent home. Even though I had my extended family around me, I still had a rebellious spirit all together toward my mom and felt as if she was holding me back. A few months after calling it off with the older guy I had been dating, I went to a party with my baby sister and my best friend. My mom had said the only way my little sister could go I had to go with her and later I found out my friend would be there as well. I remember telling him I really did not want to spend my Friday night at one of my sister's friend party and was attempting to find somewhere else to go. I was secretly planning to leave my sister at the party and come back for her when it was time to go home. I remember telling my friend who the person was and he told me he was going to be there too. At that point I became confused trying to figure out how in the world was he associated with this group and why didn't I know. I asked him how he knew them and found out that the party was actually for a friend of his who stayed right up the road from his house. He convinced me to go ahead and come to the party. Making me promise I wouldn't leave. Truth was I really had no choice since he wasn't going to be home that day killing my plans on slipping away. That Friday, I really made no attempt to really fix myself up. Thinking I was going to be around a bunch of kids my sister's age. When our ride pulled up, I saw my best friend in the car, and I was over joyed to see him. I remember getting into the car and seeing that there was nothing but guys in it! Two were my silly cousins, one had begun to hang out with me and my best friend, and the others were guys I had seen hanging around my friend's house. Everyone knew that my friend and I was family, so there wasn't any confusion with the way we hung out with each other. Arriving at this house, not far from my friend's home, I remember thinking who would have ever thought a house was out there. Walking in, I thought it was really nice, but it still was not where or how I wanted to spend my weekend. Going down to the rec room, I remember thinking "wow, who would have thought this was part of the house?" There were several people there, of various ages, and believe it or not, there was drinking! I remember going over to my friend and asking him whose home was this? He started scanning the room like he was looking for someone and pointed over into a corner telling me "his." I glanced in the direction that he was pointing in and immediately my eyes were big. Who on earth was this person and how come we had never met. I remember asking my cousin who he was and my cousin looking at me with this smirk on his face asking me why? The look I gave him was enough for me to get the answer to the question. Asking more questions, I found out they were really close, so I informed him to introduce us. I remember my friend looking at me and quickly pulling me to the side as if he didn't want anyone to hear what we were saying. He asked me was I sure and I gave him the curious look. Trying to figure out why he asked this question. He looked at me and plainly told me that I am his cousin, this is his friend, for him this was a bad combination. At first, I really could not understand why my friend was suddenly so serious, but realized after that comment what he was trying to say. I did assure him that he would not be caught in anything that took place between me and this guy. Letting him know I would not do this to him. He gave me this puzzled look as if I said something really stupid and quickly let me know that it didn't matter. If the guy hurt me in any kind of way, it didn't matter, we were family. I remember smiling and hugging him so hard. Truly I have a really good friend and this touched my heart to know he cherished our relationship as much as I did. Afterwards, I convinced him to go over and inform this friend of me. Ensuring I gave him some good words to describe me with. I remember him giving me this disgusted look while walking off attempting to remember my words. Standing in the corner, I watched as they spoke. Wondering what was being said and what would happen. Looking back now, I really believe my friend stalled in the beginning because of how they were just standing there laughing. After a while, I started getting upset because I really felt like he was not going to introduce me. Right when I started to get up and go outside, I saw my friend point over at me. I remember thinking, "oh my God, did he really just point toward me?", causing the guy to glance over in my direction. When we looked at each other, he smiled at me and said something to my friend. I stood there holding my breath and about to pull every stand of hair out of my head. My friend took forever ending the conversation just to come back and tell me what was said. It's funny how teenagers go on when they see someone they would like to get to know. Always wondering what the other person is thinking, but too afraid to get that answer. Youth is truly an amazing point in life. Much is learned through the process of going through, but it also brings a desire for more. After a while, my friend walked back over toward me, but he had to stop to speak to everyone in between. By the time he got to me, I was fuming. Seeing I was mad, he deliberately took his time relaying any message and laughed when I promised him I was about to sock him a good one. Once he calmed down, he did relay the message and my anger quickly turned to a smile. A few minutes later, the same person I had admired across the room walked over and asked me to dance. At that moment, I was glad I went with my sister and had a lot of fun. When you're the older sibling, you don't believe the younger group have that much fun, but who would have known. From that night forward, this new guy and I talked all the time over the phone. There were those nights we talked until the next day; causing us to sleep later on many occasions. I remember my friend calling me one Saturday and asking me why I hadn't been out there. I really couldn't give him a good answer and he became upset with me. After we talked, I told him I would come out there that day. I really didn't want to spend my day at home and plus I hadn't seen him in a few weeks. Making it to his home, I could tell he was happy to see me and I really missed him too. We sat around talking, catching up on some stuff, and pretty much clowned around for the day. Not long before I was about to go home, my new boyfriend and some of our other friends came out to his place. I remember smiling, happy to see him, and thought that the day was ending perfect. I remember looking at my friend and seeing that his face had changed somewhat. I asked him what was wrong, he told me nothing, but there was a dryness there where it didn't use to be. I watched him closely, as he interacting with everyone, but there was something different with his interaction with my boyfriend. I couldn't put my finger on it, but something was definitely up. With this in mind, I had every intention to investigate. Driving me home, I remember approaching him again and again he continued to say everything was okay. Looking at him, I explained we were still friends and he could tell me anything. Pulling up in my yard, I gave him this look waiting to see if he would come out with it. He smiled, told me to tell "momma Becca" hey and pulled off heading back home. Walking into the house, it still bothered me that there was something going on that I didn't understand. I couldn't put my finger on it, but eventually I stopped trying to guess. Some weeks later, my boyfriend was in a tragic accident, causing us to rush to the hospital. I was so upset and couldn't stop crying. Something always seem to come and try to steal my happiness. Later on, after making it home, I got a call from my friend. We talked on random things and laughter was distant from my heart at that moment. After a while, he asked if he could come over to talk to me about something and, of course, I agreed. I believe, at that moment, I thought something was wrong with him and decided to be that friend he needed me to be. He was in between girlfriends and knowing him another one was in the mix. I remember shaking my head and preparing for "the talk" I always managed to give him about this. Little did I know it wasn't me that would be doing the talking, but a friend being exactly what he was at that moment. A friend. Hearing his loud engine roaring up, I opened the front door and walked out on the porch. It was a cool, beautiful night, so I figured this was better than being cooped up in the house. Walking up on the porch, he asked me where was my mom and I pointed toward the house. Going in, he walked straight toward the den, stuck his head in the door, and spoke to everyone like he normally did. With my mom, it was always different. For some odd reason, he loved aggravating her. The weird part about this was, my mom would act as if she was annoyed, but I think she loved when he did this. After they had their warped conversation, he walked outside where I was laughing. I remember shaking my head at him and asked him did he want to stay outside. Honestly, that was the best placed to talked, so nosey people wouldn't "accidentally" over hear our conversations. It's true younger siblings could be a pest. We had small talk for a few minutes and eventually he became quiet. Causing me to look at him, ready to give him our normal "the talk." What came out of his mouth next really shocked me and left me unprepared with words to say. "He's not faithful. He's messing around with someone else," never once turning his head. Causing me to stare at his profile in complete dread. I didn't have to ask who. I didn't have to hear the name. I knew the answer without him having to say. "I told you, you're my family. I couldn't keep this a secret, not from you. What do you want me to do?" Smiling, I looked at him and told him nothing even though I didn't mean it. I wasn't going to have my friend, my family get into trouble for me and loose a friend. He asked me was I alright, I told him yes. He explained that my boyfriend didn't know he was telling me. He wanted to be sure that my friend was not going to say anything to me, my friend convinced him he wouldn't, but in the end he came to me with the truth. I remember feeling hurt, feeling pain, but most of all rejection. My self-esteem took a hard blow and it was something I had gotten use to feeling. After a while, my friend went home. Promising he would call when he made it. Walking back into the house, I remember listening to my family in the den watching some program, but at that moment I felt completely alone. Loneliness is a feeling that can permeate every corner of the heart. Leaving so much ache, so much hurt. It has the ability to take on a life of its on if properly handled or control. At that point in my life, loneliness was quickly manifesting a friend and that friend would be called revenge.

9

Chapter Nine

Illusions are the one thing that magicians use to fascinate the people they entertain on a regular basis. They gain the attention of the people by creating a perception and distorting the end results through the illusion. At the end of the show, the audience is left in wonder how were they able to complete the trick. Some going as far as to recreate the moment in an attempt to get the answer. When one really consider the principal point behind what the magician does, one can connect this same illusion to how they have viewed the situations surrounding their lives. When the expectations of the end become completely different from what they dreamed or dare say hoped. In this place, I found myself on several occasions without truly understanding how. My thoughts always pondered what it was about me that brought about more unhappiness than anything else. I often stared in the mirror attempting to find the answers. Wondering if the reflection had them there. Was it something I was saying or could it possibly be the way I thought? I couldn't figure it out no mattered how much I stared and so, I began to close my heart. What was the point in being good to others when it only brought about more heart ache and pain? What was the purpose behind being the nice guy when others only continued to walk over you? The peers I so desperately desired to fit in with always let me know that I didn't. Much of what I knew as hope was slowly fading; being erased from me. At that point, I stopped caring. I remember after finding out the truth about my then boyfriend, I begin to state it didn't matter a lot. I remember telling my best friend I'm going to start acting like you guys. Just not caring how I treated any of the guys I met. My heart was hurt and in my mind enough was enough. I remember him looking at me and telling me not to be like that. That maybe I should just move on. Moving on was the last thing on my mind for in many ways, I really liked this one guy. It is amazing how one is attracted to what they are used to and do not realize their true worth. I didn't say anything for a long while. Still seething on the inside and ignoring what my friend was really saying. There was so much hurt in my heart. Like hundreds of knives ripping it to shred. Leaving pieces in the place where a heart use to be. I wanted to be cold. Wanted the bitterness that it brought. I didn't want to feel any forms of remorse for anything I did. I remember going about my days in school flirting and acting indifferent. Hiding behind what was truly going on in my head. I still took my boyfriend at the time phone calls and pretended just as he did. I would throw out little hints letting him know I knew, but he continued to act as if I didn't. After a while, I did meet another guy. Someone my best friend introduced me to. I remember school releasing for the day and sitting under the tree outside waiting on the bus with my friend. He sat next to me laughing and playing along with watching my reactions while he did. I knew he was wondering if I was still upset with what he shared with me and concerned about the reactions his words had. I remember looking at him, giving him that silent I'm okay, and laughing along with everyone else. I remember these particular two guys who were going out of their way to get my attention. I looked at my best friend and my looked asked a question. He quickly caught on and began to laugh. He let me know right then which one was the better choice and I looked at him. Thinking I really wasn't thinking about another relationship. For several days, this was the normal setup for after school fun with me and my friend. Staying after school until his bus showed up and walking home sometimes alone. One particular evening, my best friend informed me he was coming to my house after school. I was so happy to spend that Friday with him, but had no idea we wouldn't be alone. Meeting up that evening, I found out that the same two guys bidding for my attention were also walking the same way. One was going over family, but the other was going with my best friend. Walking and talking I really had a lot of fun. I was not thinking about the bruises I was still nursing. Not allowing the wound to determine my day and finding myself actually having fun once again. My best friend nudged me on several occasions nodding his head in the other guy's direction. At one-point whispering "he really likes you" and giving me the thumbs up for the go ahead. I remember looking at him like he had lost his mind, but at the same time began to think why not? Who exactly was I being faithful to? That was the one thing that I prided myself on and yet had not found anyone who felt the same way. It's amazing how even the young find value in that one area without one being taught it. Slowly I began to open up to this new guy and eventually I became comfortable with him. I remember us making it to my house and spending the remainder of the day just having fun outside. Soon my best friend's mom came to pick them up and being surprised to see the other guy there as well. When she addressed him, I was really surprised. He was her nephew! My best friend's cousin and they planned the entire day for him to get to know me. The look of shock was not just on my face, but also deep in my thoughts. I looked at my friend and he gave me a big smile. Informing me he would call me later. Before walking to the truck, his cousin looked at me and asked me was it okay if he called? At first I hesitated knowing that he may hang out with my not yet ex, but in the end I did give it to him. I was never the one who tried to deliberately hurt someone and wanted that same respect for myself. As I walked into the house, it was the one thought that was very persistent. I had to make a decision and quick. When I talked to my best friend, I explained all this to him and as always he just listened. When I finished talking, he gave a long drawn out sign and asked me why was I still concerned about my not yet ex's feelings. He gave valid points why I should move forward and just end it without dragging it on. Letting me know that if I tried to do it any other way, the end results would be getting a name I did not deserve. I knew he spoked the truth in everything he said, but still a part of me did not want to. I was still mad still angry from what he had did and had not let go of the past even though it was much needed. I agreed with my friend to give this cousin a chance and he assured me I wouldn't regret it. In all honesty, this I wasn't so sure of. I began talking on the phone with this guy and he started hanging out at my best friend's house with us as well. In many ways, this relationship was different and also interesting as well. We never officially stated we were dating, but in some ways those words were not needed. I started going out to his folks house many times and he would come by when he could. Eventually it led to us always being around each other and my best friend was included as well. I remember my best friend saying to me "See I told you y'all would work" and smiling as if he accomplished something huge in that statement. I remember smiling and punching him in the arm, but I did not disagree with what he said. I was happy and with someone who actually expressed the same interest I had begun to express. Being a teenager at that moment was holding a satisfaction at that moment. Dating and actually being happy with it. I was more into school, knowing he would be there, and having some great friends in the midst. School was beginning to wrap up and summer vacation was on the horizon. Many weekends were spent planning what and how it would be spent. Majority thinking, we would all be together. We already knew before we could do anything we had to do our daily chores. Even in that time, the phone was the next best course and three-way calls was a must. It was never tiring talking to everyone and if one was missing we felt it. Eventually the last day of school came and summer had officially begun. This time for me, it held much more meaning to it and I had plans on enjoying every moment of it. I remember some people I knew throwing a party and my best friend, as well as my boyfriend, being part of it. They had formed a group, during that time that was the thing, and every one of every age being there too. I remember going to the party with my boyfriend and having so much fun with him. I did notice, on several occasions, that some of the girls I thought were my friends acting distant from me. Deliberately calling on him and pulling him away. At one point, I walked out of the party and my best friend noticed. Following me and asking me what was wrong. After I explained to him what was going on, he put his arm around my shoulder and let me know it was jealousy. To not allow those things to bother me. He assured me his cousin was faithful and the only thing he talked about was me. Not long after this comment, my boyfriend came outside and that is where we stayed until I went home. There were several other summer parties, I participated with and it was a great time for me. In a few couple months, I would be turning 17 and 16 had not been all that bad. I had a great friend and my boyfriend was sweet. I was actually happy with what was going on despite the things that were trying to be negative. At that moment, none of those things mattered and I was happy with the little bubble that had formed right then in my life. About a month later, I went to another part the same group gave and this time something was different. I was told by several people I had put on some weight and in all honesty, even I had noticed. Two weeks later, it was beginning to bother me because I couldn't understand what was going on. After a while, I started noticing that something was missing. Something that never missed a month in showing up. I remember calling one of my then friend and telling her what I was thinking. She came by my house, picked up some money from me, and went to buy what I was too afraid to be seen getting. When she came back, she came into my room and told me to call her when I knew. I remember going into the bathroom, opening up the bag, and pulling out the pregnancy test in it. I was so nervous and afraid. Trying to wrap my mind around the situation. There was no way I was pregnant no way! At that moment, fear of the possibility was staggering. After reading the instructions, I proceeded to take the test. Attempting to do what the complicated directions were telling me. Gathering all the materials up, I looked around to make sure I removed everything. I knew no one should find what I was doing and if they did...I didn't want to think about it. The information stated it would take about 15 minutes before I knew the results and my nerves were so very bad. I remember lying down and closing my eyes. Before I knew it, I fell asleep. Waking up 30 minutes later, immediately my mind fell on the test. Jumping up, I ran to my dresser praying with everything in me let it not be. Looking at the test, my heart began to drop and I quickly grabbed the instructions. Glancing over it again, I looked for the results indicator with tears in my eyes at that point. I remember dropping to the floor and shaking my head. It couldn't be! Not me! I picked up the phone, called my friend girl again, and told her I messed it up I need another one. She came by again picking up the money and bring another test for me to take. Taking the second test, I was too nervous to fall back asleep, and waited to see what this one said. I sat there, attempting to will the test the other way. Afraid for several different reasons. Once the time was up, I checked the results, and again received the answer I couldn't deny. After a while, I called my youngest aunt and asked her to come over. She asked me why, but I just continued to ask. At one-point begging and crying quietly. When she came, I asked her to lock my door and showed her the two tests I had taken. She looked at me and asked me how long? That answer I did not have. She hugged me and told me not to cry. Asking me had I told my mother yet. I told her no and she just looked at me then finally stated she would do it. She sat in my room, made a doctor's appointment for me, and told me not worry myself or I will become sick. She explained to me she would take me to the doctor and then we would talk to my mom. Explaining to me the importance of staying calm. I could hear the words, see her mouth moving, watching her as she left out the room, but the numbness over my body was great. I sat there for a long while, staring at the door, attempting to wrap my mind around everything. Understanding was the last thing coming forward. How could this happen? What was I going to do? These were only some of my many thoughts at this point. Glancing outside, I saw it was night and wonder when would the light finally come in. It's true that a shock to the system can throw off everything and takes a while to recover. Everything had changed in the course of a summer and everything I knew was going with it. A fear of the unknown was before me and I didn't know what it would bring. The only thing I knew was I couldn't hide the truth even though I did not know all it would unfold in its making. To this thought, I didn't know if I should breathe for fear it would eventually stop.

10

Chapter Ten

In all things, there is a reaction that comes with it. Whether the reaction is big or whether it is small, something manages to always follow behind what is done. The question that comes behind it is often, at that moment, the one a person can overlook until later in life. This is something I can truly say I experienced on several occasions in this life I have lived. Even at the age I am at now, I find myself posing the question that I should have asked then now. I use to wonder why didn't I ask the right question then? At this point, I found the answer to that simple question. If I had asked the right question then would I have been in the right state of mind, or right state of maturity, to truly understand the answers that came from it? Or would I have missed the gravity of what this spiritual insight has granted me now to pass on to others? Many times, the point of missing in one state of mind is the ability to gain records of details we obtained throughout the years. This is a place that many people are positioned for before that transition into maturity. It's the place we occupy in that space in between maturity and wisdom that we come to value in preparation for knowledge. Being young, one can gain many things whether good or bad. It's what we do with it that determines just how much of each a person withstood in their attempts to stand. Finding out I was pregnant was a very hard situation for me to understand. I knew how it had happened, knew why it happened, but grasping me being the one was hard to accept. I was slowly falling into a deeper depression. One that combated my self-esteem, self-worth, and mind-frame altogether. I knew I had to eventually tell my mother, but that was something I did not want to do nor looked forward to. My aunt had told me to wait until we went to my doctor's appointment and she would tell her for me. I knew she was being helpful to me. Being that she experienced the same thing as a teenager herself. After going to my appointment, it was confirmed that I was pregnant and was entering into my second month. I was told that I was threatening miscarriage and it was best for me to take it easy. I remember thinking that it was due to my fear of telling my mother and my boyfriend at the time. The crazy part about this entire situation was I was more afraid of telling him and his mother than I was of anything else. I had witness what goes on when one of my peers had babies and the next thing you knew all kinds of stories were circulating the schools about them. Shredding their reputations and causing others to avoid them like they had the plague. The baby's father leading the groups that tore down the girls and others joining in with it. This was something I did not want to go through and it worried me non-stop. At one point, I became sick with stomach cramps causing my aunt to talk me into calming down. Pulling into the driveway of my house, my aunt asked me was I ready to tell my mom? I remember looking at the house I lived in and thinking I don't want to go in. After a few minutes, we got out the car with my aunt leading the way to the front door. I walked into the living room, sat in the chair next to the front door thinking if anything happened the door was right there. My aunt walked through the house looking for my mom. After finding her, she asked her to come to the living room, and they both walked in with my aunt closing the door behind them. My looked at me, then my aunt, and sat down on the couch watching us both. At that point, my mind slipped somewhere else. Not willing to be a part of the interactions. I remember hearing my aunt say I had something to tell my mom and looking at me edging me to say what it was. I stared at her as if she was speaking another language and the next thing I knew I was crying. My mom gave an irritated sigh and looked at my aunt. Demanding to know what was going on and what did I have to say. My aunt looked at her, told her "she's pregnant, and walked to stand in between us. I remember my mom jumping up and immediately going off. Exactly the reaction I was expecting. My aunt did not move from her position, but told her she needed to calm down. Explaining to her that it is done, there's nothing we could do, and then explaining the condition I was in at that moment to miscarry. My mom did not say anything more, but walked out the room without speaking. My aunt looked at me and asked was I okay? Watching me closely as I nodded my head even though I felt like there was a huge brick in my throat. She walked me to my bedroom and advised me to lay down. Telling me she would call and check on me later. After she left my room, I remember staring out the window. Knowing I still had to make a phone call. I sat there for so long that I never realized when I dozed off. A while later, a knock on my door woke me up and I sat up telling whoever it was come in. I watched as my little cousin walked in and asked me point blank was it true I was having a baby. I told him yes and the next thing I knew he was grinning big exclaiming "cool"! Telling me he would help me with everything. I remember being so overwhelmed at that point. He was the first one to actually show a different reaction than what I had been seeing so far. Even though my aunt helped me, there was a look of not surprised on her face. This made me feel as if it was expected. At the doctor's office, they made me feel worst by the looks of disdain they gave me while I was there. My mom's reaction was anger with no signs of sadness. My little cousin was the first one to actually show something that made me feel like he really cared and for the first time in days, I smiled. He then started asking me questions about whether it was a girl or boy and what was I naming he/she? I remember looking at him and telling him I did not know anything yet. Assuring him when I did he would be the first to know and watched him leave out my room grinning from that information. Watching him close the door, I sat back still smiling from his reaction. Glancing down at my stomach, it dawned on me at that moment that there was another person growing in there. I remember putting my hand on my stomach and closing my eyes. Imagining that I could see this small form within me. I felt a warmth come over me in this moment and I knew despite what was going on, everything would be alright. Opening my eyes, I took a deep breath as I reached for my phone. Staring at the numbers as I prepared to dial the number I had dreaded all day of calling. Listening to the phone ring, I rehearsed in my head what I would say and how I would tell him. Hearing his grandfather answer the phone, I asked to speak to him and waited for him to get on the phone. When he got on the phone, we talked a little bit and finally he asked me what was wrong. Closing my eyes, I spoke the words I had rehearsed over and over again in his ear. Waiting to see what his reaction would be. For only a minute, he was quiet, but to me it was an eternity. I started to wonder was he still there until he quietly asked me was that the reason I had went to the doctor and I answered yes. He was quiet once again, but after a while he assured me he would be with me all the way. At that moment, I was so relieved by his comment that I just sat there on the phone and wept. Hearing me crying, he didn't make fun of me. Just continued to talk and reassure me everything would be okay. So much pressure fell off me at that point and after a while, we just talked. We had acknowledged the situation, but we did not stay on that subject. We talked on other things like we normally would, but that situation was forever before us. A while later my phone beeped and I answered the call to hear my best friend's voice. I had already shared with him what was going on and confirmed to him what the doctor had stated. Again I had a comforting friend and reassurance that I would be okay. Smiling and crying, I placed him on the call with my boyfriend. Enjoying the conversation we were having. After a while, I told them I was getting off to go to bed. Making arrangements to go to my boyfriend's mom to inform her of the pregnancy. Hanging up the phone, I walked to the bathroom preparing to take my bath before bed. Looking in the mirror, I could still see the sadness there, but I was not going to let that overcome me. After taking my bath, I walked back to my room and immediately my phone rung. Answering it, I heard the voice of my best friend, asking me am I really okay? Smiling, I assured him I was and not to worry about me. Letting him know I believed everything would be okay. My friend was quiet for a moment and the next words he said were the words I knew would come up. The one thing that I had tried not to consider even though I knew it was there. Sitting on my bed, I answered his question despite my thoughts. How could I tell my boyfriend that I wasn't ready to be a mother and had considered abortion? To be responsible for another person was something I knew I couldn't do and the support was not where I really needed it to be. Never expecting something like this to come up. Sitting on the phone with my best friend, the one who knew so much about me, but at that point had no answers to help me. Hearing him assure me that my boyfriend would be a good father and not to let what happen blind me to that fact. Even though he was comforting me as a friend, we both knew the facts. It was something I had to deal with, no matter the consequences, and at this point it was time for a deeper breath.

11

Chapter Eleven

The one thing that is ever constant in a young person's mind would be the fact that one day they will be an adult and able to make their own decisions. Constantly hoping for the time to come when they do not have to listen to what is being told to them. What they do not realize would be that part does not necessarily change for them. Someone is always going to be there to direct them whether it is something they receive or not. Usually it does not take them long to figure this out, but there are those moments when it does. Guidance is a gift of wisdom given to certain individuals. Truly a blessing in disguise if we were to really examine its significant for each of us. It is the one thing that sticks out of everything else we encounter in this process called life. It allows us to fall back on what was passed down and helps us to make the correct choices. In many cases, it is ignored for a moment, but it is a definite revelation in the right season when it is needed. The early parts of my pregnancy was filled with nothing, but sickness on a regular basis. I had completely lost my appetite and nothing appealed to my stomach at all. At one point, I cried all the time due to being this ill and never feeling well. Every visit to my doctor was a plea for something to make me feel better, but eventually nothing worked. Leaving me to suffer through this until it got better. By the time I made it to my fifth month, I was barely seeing my boyfriend and barely talking to him. I would tell anyone who answered the phone when he called to tell him I was busy, gone, or sleep. Avoiding him at all cost. In those moments, I had no desire to be around him and seeing him caused me nothing, but anger. I didn't know why I felt this way toward him and during those times, I didn't care. I remember my mom actually feeling sorry for him and telling me not to do him that way. For a brief moment I was shocked she was saying that and it did cause me to invite him over that day. When he showed up, I knew he was happy to see me and really was interested in how I was feeling. I answered his questions and really wanted to be nice to him; but eventually I couldn't. There was this deep resentment in me that wanted to blame everything on him. After a while, I stopped pretending and told him I was ready for him to leave. I remember seeing the hurt on his face and how he quickly played it off. Not one time did I feel sorry for how I was acting and in all I honesty, felt some happiness in for what I did. After he left, I called my best friend to inform him about what had taken place. I really thought my best friend would understand what had happened; instead he tore into me. He let me know that the person I had become was nowhere near the person he knew and I was completely wrong in my actions. Letting me know that I would regret how I was treating my baby's father and eventually he would get tired of it too. I remember thinking that my friend was wrong and how could he take up for someone else. Feeling angry at this point, I let him know I had to go. Not even giving him the chance to say good-by, I hung up the phone right then and there. Staring at my wall, I felt completely alone and misunderstood by everyone. I got up, walked into the den where my family was, dropped at my mom's feet, and began to cry right there with my head on her lap. I had tried being strong during this entire time, but the stress of the situation had taken its toll. That moment, I just wanted to feel secure.

Feel some form of protection, a little self-worth. I just wanted someone to say it's going to be alright, but this I never got. For a while, I walked around with a hollowness inside that I couldn't shake no matter what I did. It was there when I woke up, when I went to school, and when I laid down in bed. Around my sixth month, I had to be removed from school due to being ill all the time. There were moments that any movements I made caused my stomach to heave throughout the day. I lost so much weight during that time and the doctor was concern for both me as well as the baby. He gave me an ultimatum right then and there. Letting me know if I did not make an attempt to eat or drink something, (regardless of it coming back up), he would place me in the hospital and feed me though an IV if necessary. Telling me that something from what I ingested would remain in my system, but I had to try no matter what. I believe he knew that it wasn't all pregnancy that was making me ill at that point. That there were things going on, along with my pregnancy, that were causing my "morning sickness" to linger throughout the day. I knew he was right about the situation and I knew I couldn't go on like I was. I knew that if I didn't start eating some form of food, get some kind of nutrition, that the little girl I had come to find out I was having would not make it into this world to experience it. Mentally I knew I what I had come to think. I knew how I felt about this entire situation. Then something happened. Something that caught me off guard and left me in total wonderment. A small movement! A tiny flutter in the lower right part of my abdomen. Holding my breath, I waited to see if it would happen again or was it just my imagination? The next thing I knew, it happened again! This time it felt stronger. As if the baby herself was letting me know she wanted to stay with me. I felt this flood in my heart like I had never felt before and I decided to try anything so that she could. I laid everything else aside and completely focused on trying to eat. Drinking a lot of ginger ale and sprite in an attempt to keep as much of it down as I could. Crackers became my best friend at some point, but eventually my body stop rejecting. I wasn't in school any longer, but I couldn't worry about that. My relationship with my baby's father was practically over, but that was another area I couldn't focus on as well. Slowly I was accepting my situation and as this happened a new feeling took its place. I didn't know what the future held for me and this child I was having. The only thing I knew was I would try as much as I could to be a good mother, but I knew that few were in my corner with that thought for me. The one thing I have come to know throughout this life from various experiences, you never know how strong you are until you're positioned to see. Once you get a clear view, it allows one to expand their lungs and prepare to receive a breath you have never experienced or knew.

12

Chapter Twelve

On Feb. 20, 1992, I woke up with a small pain in the middle of my back something I should have been used to, but there was something different with it. I rolled over onto my back and laid there looking up at the ceiling. Reflecting back over the past several weeks and truly came to term with everything that had happened. I was no longer in a relationship, but it did not disturb me as much as I had thought it would. There had been a lot of decisions made over the course of time during my pregnancy and I was completely satisfied with how everything had turned out. Closing my eyes, I contemplated on what the future would bring. If I were to believe the things going on around me, I would have to accepted I was going nowhere in life. It was something that was slowly coming into reality, but there was still this fight in me that refused to accept defeat. After a few minutes of lying there day dreaming, the pain in the middle of my back increased. At which point, I decided to get up and move around thinking this will help it to decrease. After fixing myself up, I decided to take my daily walk to the store right around the corner. I had come to crave sweets like crazy. I would normally buy a bag full to cover me for a couple of days, but ended up going right back the next day for something different. Informing my grandmother I was walking down to the store, I headed out the back door toward the path leading to my favorite place at the moment. As I walked down the path, I noticed that the pain in my back seemed to be increasing. It wasn't too bad, but it was causing an uncomfortable pressure that seemed to be engulfing my abdomen. I figured at that point, I would just walk up to the stop light then revert back toward the store before going home. I had been advised by my doctor to do some small distant walking to help with labor. In the back of my mind I thought if he had to carry the load I was carrying on a daily basis as well as trying to walk with it, he would look at himself in the same mannerism I was looking at him at that moment. Even though I could not conceive the thought of trying to walk under all that weight, I did manage to inspire myself by walking right to the small grocery store right next door to my neighborhood. Small reward for a daily task I must say. I remember walking into the store and going straight to the candy isle. The cashiers had gotten so used to seeing me that they instantly spoke whenever I enter the door. I was bending grabbing my normal sweets when a sharp pain hit across my stomach. It caught me off guard to the point I ended up leaning into the section. The clerk, who was assisting another customer checking out, noticed my stance and asked me was I okay? I assured her I was after a moment and decided to check out with less than what I would normally buy. I walked out the door still pondering the pain I felt and slowly worry started to creep into my thoughts. I didn't know if I had over done my walking the past few weeks, so decided not to walk anymore for the day. I walked as quickly as I could back to my home, but tried to be careful in the process. Walking back through the path, I saw that my mom's car was in the driveway. Feeling a small measure of relief, I stepped through the backdoor and heard her inside the den with the rest of the family. Glancing into the room, I informed her that I had a strong pain hit my stomach, but so far it had not happened again. She told me not to go too far from the house and let her know if it happened again. I agreed not to, but decided to go visit our neighbor across the street for a little while. Our neighbor was a little elderly lady who was very sweet, but at the same time direct in what she had to say. I enjoyed sitting talking with her, gaining wisdom from the things she shared with me about the times when she was growing up. I have always been drawn to the elderly and loved sitting listening to them as they spoke about historical moments or things that happened to them in the town we resided in. Knocking on the door, I felt another pain hit my stomach and this time there was a little more strength to it. The pain in the small of my back had gradually returned as well. Frowning a little, I walked into my neighbor's house and immediately started smiling. After checking to see if she needed anything from her kitchen, she informed me she had some cake in there for me and told me to go get it. I smiled and told her thank you as I went into the kitchen. Trying to figure out a way of declining it without hurting her feelings. Though she was a sweet, as well as blunt, little lady; everything she cooked always tasted like boiled chicken. The cake was no exception. I wrapped it in some paper towel and told her I would save it for later due to my stomach pain. Never had I felt so much relief with having a valid reason from eating it at that moment. I sat there with her for a while just listening to her tell me her stories when another pain, more intense, ran across my abdomen. This time, the baby reacted to the pain causing even more discomfort to take place. I could literally feel her balling up causing the pain to feel like an enlarge cramp. I lean backwards and closed my eyes. All the while rubbing my stomach thinking somehow this would stop the pain as well as the discomfort. My neighbor looked me over and asked me how long have I been feeling this way? I admitted to her I woke up with a backache that has intensified and now these pains were starting. Causing the pain in my back to grow and making me feel like my entire spine was hurting. She told me right then to get up and go get my mother to take me to the hospital now. Looking at her, I realized right then that the reality of becoming a mother was there. Going back across the street, I could hear her shouting take it easy as I moved across the street. Smiling, I knew if it was possible for her to go with me she would have. For that I was very grateful in her participation of that moment. Reaching the den, I walked in and informed my family I believed I was in labor. My mother, who was watching her favorite soap opera at the moment, eyed me and told me to sit so she could keep an eye on me. For several moments, everyone was watching me out of the corners of their eyes. As if they were expecting something tremendous to take place right there. Personally, I felt like an experiment that was under observation. Waiting for the next transition to take place. After the third pain hit after se many minutes, my mother jumped up and said let's go. If it wasn't for the pain I was under, I would have rolled over laughing at everyone. Someone had called my youngest aunt informing her that I may be in labor. By the time the third pain had hit me, she was literally sitting in a chair staring me right in the face analyzing every look I made. Making it to the car, everyone was trying to get into one car. Some kind of way everyone fit and we were off to the hospital. After getting situated in my room, I was ready to put each and every last one of them out. My two aunts stood behind the doctor as he checked me causing me to laugh despite the pain. At one point, the doctor informed me that my baby's head was stuck on the right side of my abdomen. He then let me know he would allow her to turn on her own, but he would proceed to take her due to her size. When I heard this, fear crept across my heart. Never did I think I would have to go through that procedure. Holding my hand, he told me it would be alright and to try to get some rest. At that moment, I understood how fear could take shape and form. Not knowing what the initial outcome would be and succumbing to even more pressure of self-esteem. To me, it was my fault this was happening and

I was paying for every mistake I had made. I had not been the perfect daughter, sister, niece, or girlfriend. The shimmer of hope was slowly fading and I waited anxiously for a sign that it would be ok. Instead I got a phone call from a family member telling me quite frankly that I was in a position where I could die. Encouragement is something many people need to receive. Even if it is just a small measure of reassurance. When it is something that is limited in its appearance, it can produce another way for the enemy to get in. A seed can be planted, whether it is good or bad, in soil that can produce. If the seed produce weed, it can cause entanglement, but the breath that comes in later determines what's meant to last. I had to continue breathing for my daughter's sake.

13

Chapter Thirteen

At 1:44 p.m. on Feb. 21, 1992, I gave birth to my firstborn through cesarean by the hands of my doctor. It was a moment that I initially slept through, but never the less, a great moment. Waking up later that day, I was introduced to her for the first time as well as a horrible pain I had never experienced before. I remember crying and telling my mom it hurt and her telling me it would get better. My first cousin and aunt were one of the first set to visit me that day. I remember putting my cousin out my room because she was having too much joy in poking fun of me My mom and aunt thought it was hilarious. As for me, I could have put them out too. I dozed off not long after that and when I woke the next time my daughter's father was sitting there. My mom told me he had been there the entire time, but each time he came in to speak I was asleep. I looked at him wondering what he was thinking, but was truly amazed at him. Here was someone I had really not been very nice too, but yet he still managed to come. I had spoken with my best friend the night I went into the hospital and he was right there within minutes. I had told him not to tell my ex I was in the hospital, but of course he never listened. He didn't tell him the night I went in after he visited, but he made it a point to contact him the day I went into surgery. I had no idea until that moment that my ex had been there the entire time. Looking at him at that moment, I couldn't do anything, but smile. My first words to him was to ask him had he ate and the look he gave me was relief. I really felt bad at that moment for how I had treated him, but thoughts of cheating came back up in me. I decided to ensure there was some distance between us due to that, but I knew I still cared about him. The next day, the doctor told me I had to get up and walk; despite how I was feeling. I remember thinking he has to be crazy. There was absolutely no way I was moving and little did I know how right I was. My mom had bought me a night gown that had sparkles and designs on it. Not long after putting it on to go walking around in, I began to itch something fierce. Not long after, I realized I had some sort of reaction to the glitter and my baby did too. After removing the gown, as well as washing off, the itching did not leave, but continued. The nurses brought several different creams to try to stop it and nothing was working at the time. After a while, my nurse brought in some kind of ointment that was used for peeling skin and immediately the itching stopped. We were all shocked at how something like this was working, but relief was greatly appreciated at that point. Not long after finding comfort with the ointment, another issue quickly rose up. I remember laying there in bed watching television with my mom as she held the baby when the left side of my face started feeling funny. I felt something running down my chin and reached to wipe it off. Looking at my hand, I saw that saliva was coming out the left side of my mouth and my speech was slurred when I tried to get my mom's attention. My eye had drooped and the entire left side was completely numbed. At that moment, I became more afraid from what was happening. My mom called the nurse who quickly contacted my doctor to get him to the hospital. Not long after that, my doctor walked into the room and examine me to see what was going on. He then told me I had something called bell palsy and it was something that some women experienced after having a baby. He assured me that it would eventually go away and I would recover to my normal self. In the meantime, he wanted to keep me a couple more days to continue monitoring my condition. I remember laying there trying to absorb this information. Another medical condition coming up against me. I could not comprehend why all of this seemed to be coming against me and before I could stop it, I began to cry. Everything seemed to be happening to me. In my hope to make the best out of this situation, I seemed to be suffering even the more than I could believe. Where did it stop and the happiness began? What had I done that made even my health to go against me? So many thoughts, so many questions bombarded my mind at that point. Causing me to lose any interest to what was being said and what was being done around me. Every image in my mind was a mass of unrealistic promises and hope was the furthest thing from my thoughts. I remember my best friend coming by to see me one day. I was preparing to walk for that day and he decided to help me with it. As we walked, he made casual conversation while watching me and my reactions. Doing what he does best, being a friend. I remember telling him how I felt, about all the medical issues I was going through at that moment. He listened and asked me one question. Do you regret making your decision? I thought about that question as I walked with him up the hall. Rolling it around in my thoughts as I considered my issues. When I looked up, we were standing at the maternity ward. Looking at all the babies in the room. I looked around and found my little girl. Signaling to the nurse to pull her closer so we could look at her. Looking at her tiny figure lying there in her hospital clothing, I smiled and told him no, I didn't. At that moment, I realized that even though everything had taken place to make me view the negative, she was the breathing image of a positive. I completed something wonderful in nine months of pregnancy and nothing else I could do in this lifetime could replace that accomplishment. Kissing my friend on the cheek, I told him thank you and then proceeded to ask him to be her god father. Smiling big, he asked me who else was going to do it? I knew in my heart he was grateful. After asking the nurse could she bring my bundle of joy to my room, we finished my walk for the day. After helping me into the bed ensuring I was comfortable, my best friend went to get himself something to eat. Watching the door close behind him, I smiled for the first time in days. I grabbed hold of the little peace that had entered in after days of fear and being unsure of everything I had experienced. I looked up at the ceiling and just made one special request. I then closed my eyes, took a deep breath, and released it with the hope that the uneasiness went with it.

14

Chapter Fourteen

Ordered steps are the one thing that man is supposed to ask our God for on a daily basis. When we set aside ourselves and open ourselves to the Great I Am, impossible becomes a possibility. These are lessons that one of a young age do not always understand, but through the journey of one's life we become more willing to lean not into our own understanding. It took years for me to understand what it truly means to become a servant to another and even now I'm still learning this role in its entirety. Even though this is something I'm coming into true understanding about, during the time of growth I could not comprehend this quality; especially when I was still lost in a darkness that felt never ending during that time. After being released from the hospital, I step into the role of a mother. I had no clue to what this role really meant nor what it was supposed to exemplify, but it was something I could not back down from at this point. Reality came down with little regards toward whether I was ready, but stepping into it was immediate. So many people wanted to pry into this area, but as usual I kept many at arm length. In truth, I believe this just added gas to a fire, but reality was still something I pushed away with everything in me. As time went by, I became more and more isolated within myself. Keeping my inner demons locked on the inside and allowing them to continuously whisper within my ear. My very nature was changing rapidly and I truly felt as if there was literally nothing more that I could do. Eventually I became employed and tried to use this to support unhealthy habits I had come to depend on more and more. Desiring to drink more and more just to get pass the dreams that seemed to lurk behind my eye lids. Every day, I got up with limited motivation to go forward and every evening I wondered how I did this. I could not see the differences that were subject to be daily, only the irrelevance of them all. I knew I was suffering from depression, but had little knowledge to the extent that it shrouded me. As well as the purpose the enemy was striving to eradicate me from this world. Each day was a dream state and a nightmare I felt I would never escape. I became involve with other people who dealt in prostitution, robbery, and sold narcotics to those who were just as lost. The funny thing about this was I knew this lifestyle was not right and every time I attempted to move within it, I was kicked out for reasons at the time I could not understand. Speaking with my best friend about this, he just let me know that I wasn't happy because I was not supposed to be out there like that. That the course I was taking was not the one I'm supposed to have; especially with the fact that I had a baby. He let me know I was not a prostitute nor was I a drug dealer, but a good person doing stupid stuff. Informing me that it was time for me to get myself together. I was truly hurt from what he said, but I believe the pain was more for him saying the words versus the force that came with it. It is never easy to hear the truth from a stranger, but even more hard to take from a friend. Gradually I pulled out of that lifestyle and back into the elusiveness I had started after coming home from the hospital. A couple of months later, my friend decided to go to Job Corp and I felt as if a part of me was walking away. We both cried and hugged. Making promises to write each week until he came back and then he was gone. For a while, I was incredibly sad and hated he was gone. I believe the moment I got a letter and a phone call was the moment my spirit lifted. Eventually I got another job and gradually chose to be a little happier than what I was. It is amazing now to really experience how much energy it takes to walk in misery versus having a choice in the matter. I was still drinking, but it was not as much as what I had been doing before to my thinking.

After a few months, my best friend came home and it felt so good to have him back. Talking on the phone and writing letters kept him close, but it was much better having him right there with me. Life felt a little bit better, but as all things goes, you still must be prepared for changes to take place. Prior to his leaving, he was dating someone and he would share things with me regarding this relationship. Telling me his secrets with the belief that I would never let a word of it pass my lips. From that day to thins one, I have kept my promise and smile thinking about those long-ago conversations. Eventually he informed me he was ready to settle down and start a family of his own. At first I laughed because I knew the characteristics he demonstrated to the world, but all along he was the sweetest person, if not warped in sense of humor, I knew. I remember thinking about how we met and also how I really did not like him at first. As time went by, we became closer and closer until we were inseparable. Practically brother and sister by default with a great love for each other. I told him I was happy for him and could not wait for him to inform the young lady he had great intentions for, but it never happened. The next day, I woke up smiling because I knew what he had plans to do and I knew that by the time I made it home from work he will have his answers. All that day, I was motivated and could not wait for the day to come to an end to get home. As soon as I clocked out for the day, I walked out the door on my way home preparing for my expected phone call (or possible a visit) when an ambulance passed me. At first I thought something had happened at the high school, but the next thing I knew I saw my best friend's face. As if he had stepped out of an invisible door just to stand in front of me and smile. At that moment, a dread hit me so hard that I could not shake it off no matter how hard I tried. I started to run as if the very hounds from hell were chasing me trying to get to a phone as quickly as possible. I do not remember how long it took me to get home. All I remember is bursting through the doors and calling out to anyone who was there had my friend called me, but there wasn't an answer to that question. Going through the house, I noticed no one was there and my little girl was gone to. Running back to my room, I grabbed my phone and attempted to call my friend. I just needed to hear his voice. I just wanted to be sure he was alright and that vision was not telling me what I was not willing to accept. After calling several times, I eventually ran up the road to a family member's house of his just to see if they had heard from him. After getting to the house, the people across the street informed me they were not home and so I turned walking back to my home with a deeper sense of please. After making it back home, I decided to call his girlfriend just to ask if she had heard from him. Once she got on the phone, I could hear the tears in her voice and immediately I chose to overlook it. After asking her had she spoken with him, she paused and cried even harder. She asked me, "has no one told you?" At that moment, that question truly confused me and I could not ask the only reply that could follow it, "tell me what." Before the thoughts could be completely comprehended, her next response has haunted me from that day until this one, "he's dead." My reaction, at this point, was not immediate. For what felt like hours, but could only have been seconds, I could only see white. The next reaction was rage, anger, and I snapped on her for saying such a lie. She did not say anything, but allowed me to rant. For that, I am truly grateful to her. When I became quiet from the shock, she explained to me what had happened. I do not remember hanging up the phone or any reactions after that. Only hearing the phone ring and my mother's voice on the other end asking me am I alright. I lost my friend, my brother, my family in one split second. It is amazing how the heart can hold so much love for a person that every beat of it makes it even stronger. Though he is a friend of my past, he is still a brother who played a great part during that time. He was one of the parts to assist in the breath I took during those days and for that I will be eternally grateful.

15

Chapter Fifteen

To be absent from the body is to be preset with The Lord. That is what many people tell each other when they have face the loss of a love one. It is the one thing they are to find comfort with and many do manage to gain a form of peace in this time, but there are those who cannot find this comfort. Many times, people use the saying that when you hit bottom the only other option is up, but this is not always the case. Sometimes the bottom becomes a familiar area and the pain that comes from the attempts to leave it can make what the enemy is continually saying more relevant to his cause. Creating an impressive illusion for one to walk misguidedly in and doing everything he can to keep them forever blinded behind his wall of lies. Until one face the true reality, everything feels like a lost cause. This is where I lived heavily for a long time with no way to come out of this place. After losing my best friend, my heart could not take the damages behind it and life became a place that I no longer felt a part of. After learning of my friend's death, I believe I gave up. I could not find any values or any reasons for this hypocritical life that I made myself live in daily. I had a daughter, but to me, she would be much better off than having one so pathetic as a mother slowly taking her down as well. I didn't see anything beyond despair and the sight was becoming uglier by the minutes. I remember sitting on my mother's porch alone and broken. Something I had come to be use to in those young years. An emptiness closed around my mind and heart causing the void I was so used to feeling to become even greater. After a while, I got up and walked to the store where I credited 2 cases of alcohol. The look on the girl's face at the register was concern, but talking was one thing I no longer felt the energy for. When she asked how was I taking these cases back, I let her know I'm walking down the road back to my home. She informed me I could not do that and she did not want me to go to jail for caring these cases down the street. I heard the logical reasoning behind what she was saying, but the depth of my pain was clouding my judgement at that moment. Right as I was about to do something very silly, someone I knew walked into the store and intervene. They volunteered to take me home to keep me from walking and helped me to the car. I was quiet on the ride there and they did not attempt to force a conversation on me. After arriving at my home, they walked me in and just let me know they were there if I needed them to be. Leaving me with my alcohol, thoughts, and lack of emotions. I remember sitting out on the porch with one case, and just opening one after the other after the other. I don't remember how long I sat like that only how quick the cans seemed to go. Opening the second case, my mother and family pulled up while I continued to sit on the porch. Looking at me, my mother didn't say anything. Just told everyone to "let her be" and walking in the door without any other comments. I remember looking at my little girl and her smiling at me. At which point, I broke down again in so much hurt that it was hard to bare. A while later, my mom left to go to her second job and I continued to sit right there in the same spot. Before leaving, she looked at me and told me to try to get some sleep before leaving for the night. I sat there a little longer and could not understand why my grief was still so very much felt after consuming so much alcohol. It was as if nothing could eliminate the pain from the positioned it had taken. After feeling as if the effects were doing nothing for me, I lost myself deeper in the pain and hurt I was going through at that moment. The only thing that was continuous for me was the loneliness that was constantly and consistent no matter how much I desired for it to leave. Sitting there, looking at the dark sky and the billions upon billions of stars that gave light to it, I compared myself to it. The only difference I could find was the light that was shining in it versus the vast emptiness that desired to be filled within me. Everything felt hollow, even shallow at that point. The longer I sat there the more discouraged I became. To the point where the next thought was whispered to me. One that was very familiar and had been a constant visitor from a very young age. Letting me know there wasn't a point in continuing. To just let it go and end it. What was the point in suffering like that? Who was it really helping and why do I keep having to walk in this? My inebriated thoughts accepted what was being said and I felt as if there was true in what this voice was saying. My daughter would be alright. My family would take care of her I was sure of it. The two people I felt loved me the most were gone and I wanted to be reunited with them to experience that love once again. My mind's thoughts were steadily being lured into a place where I was totally convinced in what that voice was saying was truth. The next steps I made signified my acceptance to what I had to do. I did not hear anything outside of what I was listening to and my course was set. Walking into the bathroom, I opened the medicine cabinet and once again took out everything I found. The one bottle I remember taking out was half a bottle of Beyer aspirin which I opened and swallowed with other pills. Walking into my bedroom, I kissed my little girl goodbye and closed the door so she would not find me first. Walking back into the living room, I opened the front door, once again glanced up at the moon, and thought this would be the last time I would gaze at it. I laid on the couch still looking at the moon and closed my eyes for what I felt was the final time. Telling God to please take me this time, don't leave me here, and slipped into sleep. When one close their eyes, what takes place after that is truly not up to them. There is always someone waiting, watching, and determining if that time has come. I do not know how long it was after closing my eyes, but to God be the glory, they did not stay close. Before I knew it, I was seeing several different spots of color behind my lids and each one pulsated brighter than the first one. Causing me to see them in their brilliance. The next thing I heard was a voice telling me to wake up and immediately I felt as if someone punched me deep in the stomach. I jumped up, ran to the rest room, and every pill I took came up! Not one had dissolved and I was in complete disbelief! I began to cry and ask God why? Why do you not want me? As I lay with my head on the toilet, I heard a small voice say very clearly, "Because I have something for you to do." Even hearing that answer did not register in one so lost, but a form of hope developed behind it. It was the last time I attempted to leave this world by my hands, but the beginning of new attempts by others.

The journey was never promised to be easy, but it was promised to be lightened during the process. Many issues can come along for one individual and the weight can feel as if it is crushing at some points during that time. When this happens, just pause for a moment and remember the breaths you took during those times. When you recognized how you inhale during those moments, you'll welcome those moments. So now just breathe.

www.ingramcontent.com/pod-product-compliance
Lightning Source LLC
Chambersburg PA
CBHW052117110526
44592CB00013B/1641